Democracy and the Policy Sciences

SUNY Series in Public Policy
Sponsored by the Public Policy Section,
American Political Science Association
Anne Schneider and Joseph Stewart, Jr., Editors

DEMOCRACY AND THE POLICY SCIENCES

Peter deLeon

State University of New York Press

Published by
State University of New York Press, Albany

For information, address State University of New York Press,
State University Plaza, Albany, NY, 12246

Production by Diane Ganeles
Marketing by Bernadette LaManna

Library of Congress Cataloging-in-Publication Data

deLeon, Peter, 1943–
    Democracy and the policy sciences / Peter deLeon.
        p.   cm. — (SUNY series in public policy)
    Includes bibliographical references (p. 143) and index.
    ISBN 0-7914-3547-4 (hard : alk. paper). — ISBN 0-7914-3548-2
(pbk. : alk. paper)
            1. Policy sciences.   2. Democracy—United States.   3. United
        States—Politics and government.   I. Title.   II. Series.
    H97.D454   1997
    320'.6—dc21   96-52831
                                                                 CIP

10 9 8 7 6 5 4 3 2 1

Democracy means simply the bludgeoning of the people by the people for the people.

—Oscar Wilde, *The Soul of Man Under Socialism* (1890)

CONTENTS

PREFACE

Ever since Harold Lasswell and his colleagues first set down the broad outlines of the policy sciences in the late 1940s, the policy sciences and their characteristic approach have been at least nominally associated with what Lasswell later characterized as the "policy sciences of democracy." Yet few visions have been so apparently disrupted—perhaps even consciously distorted—for once the policy sciences mechanisms became one of the hallmarks of contemporary governmental processes in the United States, their practice has been formidably distanced from their proscribed democratic ideals and origins. Indeed, Lasswell himself forecast this possibility when he presciently warned that left unattended, the policy sciences of democracy might well become the "policy sciences of tyranny."

Some fifty years later, it would appear that the dark angel of the policy sciences seems more manifest than its fairer twin. Although some authors who have addressed this concern have concluded that it is not yet reality, others have been less optimistic and, to be fair, not often far from the mark in specified cases.[1] Liberal and conservative commentators have adopted analytic conventions to demonstrate their special points with little appreciation of Lasswell's initial idea of enhancing (as opposed to biasing) the quality of policy-making through an improved quality of information. This book attempts to trace the steady rise of this particular éminence grise to understand what brings this condition to bear and, just as important, to argue that its imminence is not necessarily irreversible within the dual guidelines of the policy sciences and democracy. The argument hopes to bind the policy sciences more clearly to the democratic processes and ethos, so that the improvement of policy research will likewise benefit the democratic system.

The careful reader will quickly discern that an important component of the analysis will somewhat deny the procedures under which

policy analysis has become commonplace in the nooks and crannies of
virtually every level of American government, most especially those
dicta relating to what philosophers of science refer to as positivism.
I prefer to alter this lens to a perspective often described as "postpositivism," for the key reason that, under its aegis, one can begin to
see the means (as opposed to the semantics) by which democratic
processes and endgame can be reinserted into the policy sciences'
approach. Secondarily, as we shall see, this perspective casts a certain querulous glance at the validity of the general positivist approach to the policy sciences, but, at least in this harmony, I am far
from a sotto voce.

   Still, I do not wish to downplay this change in perspective, for it
also indicates that part of the reason why policy sciences have become yet another vested tool for interest groups is their tradition
grounded in economics and other trappings of a positivist philosophy, whether they accept its assumptions or not. Concomitantly,
viewing the policy sciences in a postpositivist manner is to cast an
indirect but forceful vote for a wider, more liberating views than is
traditionally (and currently) the case of how one conceptualizes and
practices the policy sciences. This will almost surely involve new
ways of carrying out policy research and drawing out the inferences
and implications.

   Like so much of the policy sciences, this potential threat (and
hopefully lifeline!) might well be an idiosyncratic American phenomenon.[2] So permit me to write from an American's perspective. I do
not pretend what the following analysis portends to our (say) Dutch
or Swedish colleagues, but I would not be surprised that even with
their different political systems and polities if many of the same per-
ils endangered their particular reading of the policy sciences. And,
in any case, since the policy sciences are fundamentally contextual,
other nations must consider their own possible divergences from the
democratic tenets and make their respective adjustments. This
book, then, does not talk directly to all nations' uses of the policy sciences, let alone with their respective brands of democracy; it does,
rather, offer one possible remedy that might be useful elsewhere.

* *

   Parts of this book were first proposed in the pages of the following journal articles: "The Democratization of the Policy Sciences,"
Public Administration Review, Vol. 52, No. 2 (March/April 1992); "Reinventing the Policy Sciences: Three Steps Back into the Future,"
Policy Sciences, Vol. 27, No. 1 (1994); "Democracy and the Policy Sci-

ences: Aspirations and Operations," *Policy Studies Journal*, Vol. 22, No. 2 (Summer 1994); and "Democratic Values and the Policy Sciences," *American Journal of Political Science*, Vol. 39, No. 4 (November 1995).

* *

A number of people have been influential in helping me conceptualize this book, as will soon become apparent. Although few may choose to 'fess up, I would like to single out with great appreciation Drs. Andriana Alberti (University of Bologna, Italy); Robert B. Denhardt (University of Delaware); John S. Dryzek (University of Melbourne); Frank Fischer (Rutgers University); Hank C. Jenkins-Smith (University of New Mexico): Lawrence M. Mead (NYU); Martin Rein (MIT); Richard J. Stillman II (University of Colorado at Denver); and Douglas Torgerson (Trent University, Canada). Dr. Albert P. Williams (RAND Corporation) has always been of great assistance, even if he does not completely appreciate his contributions. Professor Linda deLeon (University of Colorado at Denver) has been a constant and simultaneous critic and supporter. Natalie Baker took precious time away from her doctoral studies to read and comment on various chapters. And, of course, Paul A. Sabatier (University of California at Davis) has been a consistent (if unknowing) source of direction (surely to Professor Sabatier's mortification). Lastly, the late Harold D. Lasswell's writings on the policy sciences are still teaching us all, if only perhaps to live with the frustration of being unable to match his vision.

I am especially pleased that this book is the initial publication in the SUNY Press series in Public Policy, for it gave me the wonderful opportunity to work with the series editor, Clay Morgan, and production editor Diane Ganeles. All authors should be so fortunate; Mr. Morgan's patience and Ms. Ganeles' redactorial diligence have made this book much more professional than might otherwise have been the case.

* *

I am finishing this book just as my wife, Linda, is preparing the documentation to support her tenure candidacy. Regardless of the outcome—which is as probabilistically assured as Michael Jordan going to the hoop—one needs to appreciate the spirit she gives so freely and so often, even in the face of her own career's hurdles. And I am endlessly grateful.

1

THE
DEMOCRATIC DREAM

Democracy is the name we give the people whenever we need
them.

—Robert, Marquis de Flers and
Armand de Caillavet, *L'Habit Vert* (1913)

The American Body Politic . . .

The predominant American political belief—attained, pre-
tended, or otherwise—from before the establishment of the Republic and throughout the nation's history has been the democratic
dream, nominally based on some version of popular representation
and governance. Virtually every political structure and reform—
from the founding Federalist Papers through the Civil War, the Progressive Era, and the War on Poverty—have been predicated on some
mode of the democratic, egalitarian ethos, even as they oscillated between its Jeffersonian and Hamiltonian poles. At least as far back
as the Boston Tea Party to the Emancipation Proclamation to Manifest Destiny and as recently as the Clinton invasion of Haiti (with
a multitude of political points in between), the United States has
initiated countless policies and programs based on the democratic
dream, deserved or otherwise.

Indeed, to imagine a widespread domestic political movement
(and probably foreign policy initiative) that does not in some very

1

visible manner drape itself in the sacred vestment of democracy is inconceivable. The Confederacy's secession was at least partially motivated by the Southerners' perception that they were being denied their constitutional, democratic rights by the dominant industrialized Yankees; the Pacific migration across the Midwest Plains and western mountains was motivated by men (and women) seeking their own democratic destinies, an option finally exhausted by Frederick Jackson Turner's declaration in the late nineteenth century of the closing of the West; and the Progressive Era, women's right to vote, and the later labor movements were heavily wrapped in democratic swaddling clothes. The First World War was declaredly fought to "make the world safe for democracy," while the Second World War was obviously a battle against brutal totalitarian governments. The 1960s brought forth the civil rights and feminist politics, both long-deferred democratic movements representative of all the nation's citizens. Even today, the dream and its enabling symbolism hardly pause: witness, for instance, how Ross Perot's United We Stand America (later renamed the Reform) party—arguably the most unabashedly centralized American political party this century—repeatedly insists on its egalitarian heritage and platform in the face of one man's Croteus-like wallet.

It is in this ambience that American political philosophies, politics themselves, and even certain professions (e.g., public administration) were created and nurtured. Although democratic proponents unquestionably argued over differing points of view (e.g., states' rights versus federal rights versus individual rights), the Constitution and its amendments have generally served as the one unifying symbol overarching the American polity and its diverse citizenry. That is, while many have debated over the duties, roles, and shape of government, few mainstream politicians have argued outside the acknowledged ken of the federal Constitution. It is, for all intents and purposes, the sacrosanct bedrock of the American democratic political system.

But the Constitution itself cannot serve as a singular political poultice for whatever ails the body politic. Part of the genius of the Constitution is that it sanctions political and social controversy without itself being tarnished. Hyperpluralism appeases the many without satisfying the nation as a whole, thus leaving a sorry residual of a government that "works" without a whit of empathy from its citizens. Within the country at large, there is a tangible sense that as often as appeals are made to the nation's democratic bench marks, these are more calls to a fading faith than references to reality.

Americans are apparently disenchanted with their politics, both in terms of substance and process.

In light of these ills, it is not surprising that Christopher Lasch, just before his death in 1994, asked the hardest question of all, that is, "whether democracy has a future." Lasch contended that "It isn't simply a question of whether democracy can survive . . . [it] is whether democracy deserves to survive."[1] This certainly is not the place to enter into that particular discussion. Just permit me to say that the overriding assumption—postulate—of this book is overwhelmingly positive in that regard for any number of normative and political reasons that one trusts most readers can appreciate on any number of levels.

Academics, as is their traditional wont, have long voiced a despair over forms and models of democracy. Benjamin Barber distinguishes, for instance, between "weak" and "strong" democracies in terms of their active voter participation rates, while others offer remedies that have little realistic chance for implementation.[2] Inevitably, popular journalists are not far behind. E. J. Dionne, as brusquely as anybody, explains *Why Americans Hate Politics:*

> At a time when the people of Poland, Hungary, and Czechoslovakia are experiencing the excitement of self-government, Americans view politics with boredom and detachment. For most of us, politics is increasingly abstract, a spectator sport barely worth watching. . . . Our system has become one long-running advertisement against self-government.[3]

Michael J. Sandel strikes much the same chord, when he writes, "Our public life is rife with discontent. Americans do not believe they have much say in how they are governed and do not trust government to do the right thing."[4]

It goes without saying that the more visible voter behavior signals this unrest. Eligible voters voting in presidential elections have fallen steadily since 1960, with only a 1992 reversal due to Perot's 19 percent of those voting violating the trend. George Bush was elected with less than half the eligible voters in his favor. Bill Clinton was even further removed from a majority in the 1992 presidential election, and the Clinton-Dole election in 1996 was conspicuously marked by one of the lowest voter turnouts of the twentieth century. Off-year elections rates have declined since 1966, with a momentary respite in 1982 (when Ronald Reagan secured a Republican Senate); of course, the absolute number of voters is much lower than in the presidential election years. Even the Republican majority elected in the 1994 elections to control Congress fell quickly out of public favor, when subsequent surveys reflected a dissatisfaction with its Contract for America as campaign promises were transformed into personal deprivations and displacements. Voter turnout statistics are even more discouraging as one moves from federal elections to those on the state and local jurisdictions. Even news viewer- and readership (probably the most painless of all democratic activities) are markedly down over the last five years (e.g., television news viewership declined from 60 percent in 1993 to a present 48 percent).[a] Most disheartening, Republicans (78%) and Democratic as well as nonvoters (both 57%) polled indicate that "government is almost always wasteful and inefficient."[5]

One can hardly compare the present protestations of citizen ennui with a nation whose establishment was based on a popular rebellion, whose most moving political event—the Civil War—was waged by large numbers of men, mostly volunteers, or one whose civil emancipation recruited millions of civil right leaders and followers into the streets and voter booths, or a nation whose labor movements were to improve significantly the quality of life for its working population. Still, we should not underestimate the disenchantment with democracy and its attendant processes and products. Robert D. Putnam has brilliantly characterized this growing sense of frustration and alienation with the revealing observation that the nation is surrendering its social cohesions (or what the sociologist James S. Coleman refers to as "social capital"), or in his words, that we are in matter of empirical fact "bowling alone."[6] Although Putnam's carefully drawn speculation does not directly indict the political system, it is scarcely idle speculation to suggest that the political system in seeming turmoil has done nothing to relieve this condition. Even worse, little better is being offered by any political party as an acceptable palliative.

Various authors have offered their "best guess" as to the source of the American malaise, ranging from race relations to a shrinkage of the middle class to the cynicism of the media to the economy to Lasch's disdain for elite behaviors to Putnam's pervasiveness of television. Whatever, this decline in American's faith in their political culture is the hallmark of the final decade of America's twentieth

---

[a] Interestingly enough, those who heard their news via radio listenership actually rose, from 42 percent (1995) to this year's 44 percent, following a five-year pattern of increased listenership.

century. Most will agree with William Greider when he writes that the resulting political insolvency is both patent and pervasive:

> The decaying condition of the American democracy is difficult to grasp, not because the facts are secret, but because the facts are visible everywhere. . . . The things that Americans were taught and still wish to believe about self-government—the articles of civic faith we loosely call democracy—no longer seem to fit the present reality. . . .
>
> The blunt message of this book is that American democracy is in much deeper trouble that most people wish to acknowledge. . . . What exists behind the formal shell is a systemic breakdown of the shared civic values we call democracy.[7]

President Clinton took up this issue in his July 1995 address to Georgetown University:

> . . . it is difficult to draw the conclusion that our political system is producing the sort of discussion that will give us the kind of results we need. But our citizens, even though their confidence in the future has been clouded, and their doubts about their leaders and their institutions are profound, want something better.

It would appear, in summary, that the uncertainties and ambiguities fostered by democracy and the democratic processes (no one has ever suggested that "democracy makes the trains run on time") are beginning to weigh heavily on the American people. For instance, the 1995 federal budget donnybrook and its poisonous reserve of rhetoric and ill-feeling between the Republican Congress and President Clinton hardly infuses any American with a glow of patriotic serenity. If it were a singular phenomenon, one might safely blame a party or individuals (and vote it or them out of office), but coming close upon a decade of Republican-bred corruption[8] and Clinton's predilection for indecision (which some wags have described as "waffling"), it is hard to accept with civic equanimity. If there is still a democratic booster, it seemingly resides, in John Kenneth Galbraith's ironic phrase, as "a democracy for the fortunate,"[9] and even that is problematic as wealthy American taxpayers leave for low-tax havens. For whatever reasons, the American citizen and occasional voter shows every indication of not being "a happy camper." What is much less clear is what is next, a general disgruntlement with a shrugging of one's electoral shoulders, or a more serious, debilitating political movement (e.g., the Freemen phenomenon).

. . . And the Study of the Public Sector

Not surprisingly, public service and public administration in the United States have shared a similar democratic coloration. From the early days of the professional public administrator—when Woodrow Wilson temporarily partitioned "politics" and "administration" into separate entities—we find a solid stream of democratic theory underpinning and underlining contemporary public administration. The obvious exception in the history of American public administration was promulgated by the so-called scientific management movement of the early twentieth century. However, its ontogeny has undergone so many populist reforms and empowerment alterations, such (most recently) as the so-called new public management of decentralization and power sharing, that its founder Frederick Taylor would scarcely recognize his administrative offspring. The "science" claimed by Taylorites has grown noticeably softer with age.

One can argue, as Frank Fischer has with great conviction, that most of the public management strategies are much less democratic than they portray themselves, perhaps even cruel charades meant to maintain ultimate managerial prerogatives and control while, paradoxically, offering little of compensating value.[10] However, the important observation is that these changing management philosophies have always cloaked themselves in the raiment of the democratic legend to substantiate an integral part of their ideology, appeal, and, ultimately, final worth. Thus, one finds bipartisan leaders of the current "reinventing government" phenomenon clothing their theories and proposals in the garments of local, that is, more democratic, control, as opposed to an equally legitimate (and often historically valid) theme of small-minded parochialism, "bossism," and local intolerance.[b] There are, it would seem, certain canons that must be honored in order to justify movements and practices in the American body politic, of which democracy is the most unwavering. The demo-

---

[b] "Reinventing" also brings with it worrisome baggage to a democratic system. Vice President Al Gore's *National Performance Review* draws a clear distinction between "citizens" and "customers," favoring the latter as a key instrument toward the revitalization of the American bureaucracy. Unfortunately, that perspective, especially as it is being implemented, destroys the role or place of citizenship in lieu of the demanding customer who can (should?) easily transfer allegiance to an alternative vendor as part of legitimate market behavior. I am indebted to Professor Laurence Lynn (University of Chicago) for pointing out this distinction to me.

cratic rhetoric is viewed as fulfilling an insistent symbolism that
must be popularly acknowledged before the managerial innovation
or political idea can be legitimated and put into place.

Much more explicitly, the newer discipline of the policy sciences
falls into much the same characterization. While the policy sciences
are characterized by some as having a long history (if they are defined in terms of advice to rulers[11]) and a short past (if they are
defined as emanating from the carnage of the Second World War as
a systematic, institutionalized approach to improved governance),
they have inevitably been alluded to as "the policy sciences of democracy." In terms of the latter definition, they were first articulated by
Harold D. Lasswell in 1949; two years later, Lasswell and Daniel
Lerner further set forth the concept of the policy sciences in their
seminal volume, *The Policy Sciences*. In Lasswell's very words, "the
policy sciences of democracy" were "directed towards knowledge to
improve the practice of democracy."[12]

Since then, the policy sciences and their more applied "kin,"
public policy analysis in its various guises, have become prevalent,
indeed, virtually ingrained in the woof and warp of government. As
Alice M. Rivlin noted over a decade ago in the midst of a Republican
administration widely thought to be antianalysis,[13] policy research
has "dramatically changed the nature of public policy debate. . . . No
debate on any serious issue . . . takes place without somebody citing
a public policy study."[14] Certainly during the current administration
headed by a president often said to be a "policy wonk,"[15] Rivlin's (formerly the first director of the Congressional Budget Office, then Clinton's director of the Office of Management and Budget, and presently a governor of the Federal Reserve Board) depiction is even
more accurate than ever. Witness, for instance, the uncountable number of "analyst-years" (to say nothing of the opportunity costs) ex-
pended by President and Mrs. Clinton on the thorny questions surrounding an American national health care insurance policy, as over
five hundred analysts worked in virtual seclusion for months to produce a universal health care proposal. But, likewise, witness the
widely held charge that the failure of the Clinton health proposal
was embedded in its closed council, nondemocratic genesis, giving
unwitting sustenance to the perception that too often important policy work is the privileged domain of distant and detached policy elite,
rather than, in Lasswell's words, one "directed towards knowledge to
improve the practice of democracy."

The present author has given voice to this sentiment when he
observed that "In the analysts' current positions (geographic and

bureaucratic), they are effectively sequestered from the demands, needs, and (most critically) values of the people they are reputed to be helping."[16] And so one is forced to wonder as to the legitimacy and validity of the so-called policy sciences of democracy or, more precisely, what they have come to be. Lasswell himself was possibly prophetic when he warned that the policy sciences of democracy could readily become, with no malice—indeed, some claim a liberal benevolence—of thought, the "policy sciences of tyranny." This caution was reiterated forty years later when John S. Dryzek wrote that "most policy analysis efforts to date are in fact consistent with an albeit subtle policy sciences of tyranny."[17] Although Dryzek was referring specifically to a potential rule by bureaucracy, there is little doubt that a ready extension of his charge could be advanced to the overall policy-making system.

Democracy and the Policy Sciences

The critical assumption for this study is that these two apparently disjoint phenomena of the decline of democracy and the rise of the policy sciences are not independent, rather, in both theory and practice, they feed upon and reinforce one another. We will attempt to propose and document that synergy, drawing upon such outstanding political scientists and policy scientists as Robert A. Dahl, Putnam, and Lasswell, to underscore that peril—although we might not know its effect or even direction—is at the door of democracy; whether today or tomorrow is less the point than its presence. Moreover, that for this malady, the remedy is critical because the game is easily worth the candle, for the "game" here is more of a threat, one that endangers the very basis of the American democratic dream and system, at least in practice. Furthermore, we choose to go beyond documenting the current peril and propose ways in which this condition may be relieved, maybe not entirely, but at least the trajectory could be lessened.

The central perspective is premised on Lasswell's original conception of the policy sciences, although this is not meant to present a Lasswellian exegesis. If not in practiced fact, then in promise, it contains the seeds for this democratic reincarnation. Concurrently, we will argue that the democratic dream itself has been misconstrued in critical ways, and transformed into priorities that only deepen rather than ameliorate the problem.

It is important to stress that this is not a chronology of American democracy, or alternatively, what James A. Morone calls *The Democratic Wish*.[18] Undoubtedly the surest way to render this book soporific would be to engage in a logorrheic debate over precisely what constitutes democracy and, concomitantly, a democratic system of government. Instead of engaging in this prototypical academic argument, we will briefly define and discuss democracy as it was originally formulated and then came to be practiced in the United States during the twentieth century, since that is the period in which we find the policy sciences being developed and disseminated, supposedly as an instrument of improved democratic governance. We need therefore to consider more precisely not only what constitutes the dream as well as how that dream came to be seen and how today it is politically interpreted and implemented.

It follows that not only will new approaches to the traditionally empirical policy sciences need to be proposed, but that adjustments to how we envision American democracy will also be necessarily relevant if we are to succeed. Joshua Cohen and Joel Rogers summarize the predicament, namely that we confront "above all an argument about democracy, the idea that free and equal persons should together control the conditions of their own association."[19] In brief, the task of this book is to reconcile the policy sciences within an expanded version of the American democratic dream so that the two work cooperatively toward mutual goals instead of being at odds with one another. Failing this purpose, it is not clear at all if either will work in their original incarnations and certainly not in harmony.

Organization

The book is divided into roughly four main sections, in addition to this introduction. The first section (i.e, the second chapter) outlines what appears to be the problems extant with the American democracy and its processes. By posing these questions, we mean to move well beyond Winston Churchill's much quoted but less-than-curative claim:

> Many forms of Government have been tried, and will be tried in this world of sin and woe. No one pretends that democracy is perfect or all-wise. Indeed, it has been said that democracy is the worst form of Government except all those other forms that have been tried from time to time. (*Hansard,* 11 November 1947, col. 206)

The reasoning is straightforward: if the admittedly ambiguous chicken entrails (or radio talk show hosts: Who can say which are better soothsayers?) are anything close to correct, democracy might still be better than "all those other forms that have been tried from time to time," but it is increasingly being removed from a workable system today. Or, alternatively, to the degree that it is workable, one might easily fear with William Greider and E. J. Dionne that it is only democratic on the margins, a mile wide and an inch deep. Michael J. Sandel, for one, presents the case that American democracy is beset with self-inflicted, internal contradictions that provide little hope for reconciliation.[20] Most of the problems addressed in this section will be of a contemporary nature. That they will be of more derivative and elaborative than original research is true enough, for most of the conditions and processes are well-known. More central to the book's theme, however, will be an exploration of the roots of American democracy and political order, traced back to the Founding Fathers (especially James Madison and *The Federalist Papers*) and the ever-observant Frenchman, Alexis De Tocqueville, with additional discussions of participatory democracy theories and movements. (One might parenthetically wonder if the framers of the Constitution themselves are icons of legitimacy, just as potent as the Constitution itself to the patrioticly inclined; consider, for one, how President Reagan favorably compared the Nicaraguan Sandinista rebels with Washington, Adams, Jefferson, and other American patriots.)

Similar explanations need to be proposed in the third chapter, that is, what ails the policy sciences of democracy and what might be a useful prescription? In brief, the issue is not so much that the policy sciences and policy analysis are quite wrong; rather, it is that in their present form and format, they are not nearly sufficient. Too many policies have been proven too far off their intended mark, so that shortcomings rather than promises are the dominant chord. In other words, important changes should be offered that would make them render them less prone to having (by now, the hackneyed charge of) "precisely the right answer for the wrong question." For one, they must face up to a situation in which the resolutions are more humanistic and less "scientific" without surrendering the requisite standards. This is less to indicate a reduction in rigor and more toward a variety of ways in which policy tools may be brought to bear for a multitude of conditions. As noted earlier, the emphasis will be toward a growing postpositivist movement, some of the obstacles it must face, and, in particular, a critical reading that will underlie the later support of participatory policy analysis as one tool in the policy sciences' methodologies.

The fourth chapter examines the means by which the policy sciences have worked to rescue their democratic charter from their insistent doppelgänger, the economics-oriented policy analysis. It reviews a number of recent advances or recommendations in policy research but, more important, it dwells to some length on some of the so-called postpositivist schools to understand what they might offer. As in earlier sections, this chapter is not meant to be the definitive statement on (say) "deconstructionism" or "critical theory" (as if either approach even admitted to such definitiveness). Rather, the chapter is intended to propose a number of theoretical insights and then to synthesize them in a manner that could lead to a more democratic model of the policy sciences than is currently the case. Admittedly (as readers of the fourth section will see), many of the postpositivist approaches have defied easy or convenient operationalization. However, this does not imply that they are irrelevant or overly "academic."

The fifth and final chapter attempts to weave these three previous sections together, that is, to advance the policy sciences in ways that they will contribute positively to the revised vision of democracy. Already some policy scientists are moving tentatively in these directions, claiming that policy should promote democratic behaviors in areas such as nonprofit organizations and local empowerment programs.[21] Still, it is apparent that these movements should be more definite in purpose and means. Furthermore, one needs to be advised how best and where to use them; if there is one lesson the policy sciences have learned, it is that there are no universal answers or omniscient hammers. Indeed, as Aaron Wildavksy warned policy analysts some years ago:

> Instead of thinking about permanent solutions, we should think of permanent problems in the sense that one problem always succeeds and replaces another . . . the capacity of policies to generate more interesting successors and our ability better to learn from them what we ought to prefer may be their most important quality.[22]

The pivotal questions thus move beyond aspirations and more into operations, for the policy sciences, if nothing else, are little without application, evaluation, and revision. Likewise, again harkening back to the original Lasswellian vision, they are empty without a democratic vision. This book attempts to correct both of these contemporary deficiencies, at least for once and hopefully for all.

2

VISIONS OF
AMERICAN DEMOCRACY

Democracy substitutes election by the incompetent many for appointment by the corrupt few.

— George Bernard Shaw, "Maxims for Revolutionists,"
Man and Superman (1903)

Introduction

The definitions of democracy are probably as numerous and flexible as any single expression in the political science lexicon.[1] Plato, in *The Republic* (book 8, 312, 558), quotes Socrates:

These and other kindred characteristics are proper to democracy, which is a charming form of government, full of variety and disorder, and dispensing a sort of equality to equals and unequals alike.

Nor have two centuries of American political philosophers and practices (as assisted, of course, by their British colleagues) helped to clarify a concept of democracy that is, nevertheless, as ingrained to the American system of government as white bread is to peanut butter.

Indeed, within the last few years, matters seem to have gotten only more ambiguous and confused. Giovanni Sartori derisively refers to a number of authors who have come to treat democracy "at whim," until, at last, Sartori claims, we live in an age of *"confused democracy"* in which democracy has become a veritable "love word."

Sartori approvingly points out that as early as 1945, Bertrand de-Jouvenel was commenting that "discussions about democracy, arguments for and against it, are intellectually worthless because we do not know what we are talking about."[2] Philippe C. Schmitter and Terry Lynn Karl are even more forthright in their criticism: ". . . the word democracy has been circulating as a debased currency in the political marketplace,"[3] as any number of "People's Democratic Republics" or, of more recent vintage, "Democratic Parties of the Left" can readily attest.

The surest way to render this book dry as dust would be to engage in an extended discussion over precisely what constitutes democracy, a democratic system of government, and the responsibilities of its representatives, bureaucracies, judiciaries, and citizens. As just implied, such definitions have consumed more thorough arguments than will be presented here. Rather than engage in this prototypical academic argument that usually engenders greater debate than clarity, let us briefly define and discuss democracy as it was originally formulated and then came to be practiced in the United States. We will finally focus our attentions largely on American politics in the latter part of the twentieth century, since that is the period in which we find the policy sciences being developed and disseminated, supposedly—but not inevitably, as we shall see—as an instrument of improved democratic communication and, hence, "better" governance.

Democracy in America

Most scholars agree that Abraham Lincoln's Gettysburg Address distilled the essence of American democracy: "a government of the people, by the people, and for the people." This description adheres naturally to the word's Greek ancestry: *demos,* "the people," and *kratia,* "to rule." But Lincoln's funeral oration leaves much to the imagination of the political theorists, such as, just who is governing whom? for whom? and for what purpose? Instead of beating each of these legitimate and justifiable inquiries to its academic death, let us tentatively accept Carl Cohen's definition—full of caveats and conditionals as it might be—as a convenient starting place:

> Democracy is that system of community government in which, by and large, the members of a community participate, or may participate, directly or indirectly, in the making of decisions which affect them all.[4]

Particular emphases should be placed on the centrality of the individual—the citizen—acting in a democratic polity, the focus of attention—the community—and the element of a democratic mode of participation. We can assume that in a system lacking any of these three components, what Cohen calls democracy itself is lacking.

Schmitter and Karl, similarly inclined, add the concepts of accountability and elections as presumed to exist, although they leave the questions of how these mechanisms operate or to what ends largely unanswered:

> Modern political democracy is a system of governance in which rulers are held accountable for their actions in the public realm by citizens acting indirectly through the competition and cooperation of their elected representatives. . . . Citizens are the most distinctive element in democracies.[5]

Concomitant with concentrating on the citizen's democratic prerogatives and responsibilities, most authors in this vein concern themselves with representation as a function of participation. Furthermore, many political observers hold that a weak (or even a tolerably quiescent) democracy can easily disintegrate into a nondemocratic, often authoritarian rule with scarcely a grumble, let alone political conflict. Without citizen concern, there is no need for representation.

The genesis of popular representation again lies with the ancient Greeks, most prominently the Athenian democracy with such spokespersons as Socrates and Aristotle. As Nancy L. Schwartz observes, "Citizens were made present in the actions of the state through an assumption of political responsibility that led them to identify part of themselves with the state."[6] A pivotal question is not so much whether democracy is participatory—no one has ever seriously questioned that assumption although the reality might be more problematic—but whether participation is manifested in a more direct (what some have called "participatory democracy") or a more indirect mode ("representative democracy"). The more decisive question is whether the size (i.e., magnitude) of the polity or citizenry *forces* the government toward the more indirect or representative pole.

During the development of the American political system, two general streams of democracy were established. The first, what Sartori calls "political democracy," largely grew out of the American political philosophy as enunciated by figures such as James Madison and Alexander Hamilton, and is most clearly articulated in *The Federalist Papers*, most particularly in Madison's pellucid No. 10. The second, which Sartori refers to as "social democracy," was originally identified with the writing of the prescient Frenchman, Alexis De Tocqueville,[7] specifically his two-volume *Democracy in America.*

The democratic yin and yang has been observed by many astute political observers. Robert A. Dahl (who has probably written more discerningly about democracy's strengths and weaknesses than any contemporary political scientist) describes these two streams in his *Preface to Democratic Theory* as Madisonian and populistic democracies.[8] Similarly, Jane J. Mansbridge (as we shall see shortly) makes an analogous division in her *Beyond Adversary Democracy* when she separates democracy into two fields, the adversary versus unitary branches. Michael J. Sandel offers a similar comparison between liberalism and a "republican political theory." The latter, Sandel holds, "means deliberating with fellow citizens about the common good and helping to shape the destiny of the political community."[9] It is necessary to explain in general what these two distinct strands of American democracy entail, both in terms of their similarities and differences, as they were originally set forth and in their more contemporary settings.

In general, Madison and De Tocqueville jointly trace their particular democratic philosophies to Montesquieu and his *Spirit of the Law* (1748).[10] They were especially traced to what Montesquieu called the "virtuous republic," and to what Richard W. Krouse later characterized as "the strict sublimation of private and particular interests to its common good or general will."[11] Although Montesquieu professed a natural (and, for his time, totally expected) sympathy with the French monarchy, he basically favored the British system of constitutional democracy and its emerging separation of powers. At the same time, both Madison and De Tocqueville shared Montesquieu's die-hard aversion to rule by an absolute monarchy or autocratic tyranny.

The key issue separating these three authors' views of the "democratic republic" was how best to safeguard democracy from various internal and external threats, which clearly reflected how Madison and De Tocqueville viewed the threats to their respective democratic angels and their resultant responses and political philosophies. Montesquieu, like Jean Jacques Rousseau and the Geneva of his *Social Contract* (1762), favored in theory a direct democracy, necessarily based on a small, more localized scale.[a] Montesquieu—who held that "it is natural for a republic to have only a small territory; otherwise, it cannot long subsist," "In an extensive republic the public good is sacrificed to a thousand private views," and "In a small [territory], the interests of the public is more obvious, better understood, and more within the reach of every citizen."[12]—was utilized by both philosophers to substantiate their arguments.

DeTocqueville drew directly from those precedents although carefully coloring his observations with the American context as he viewed it in the early 1830s, relying on what he was to call a "confederation." Madison, of course, held a markedly different perspective, one favoring a more nationalized government designed to overcome his well-known aversion to the tyranny of the majority; he was able to make his arguments persuasively before the Founding Fathers and the Constitutional Convention in the late 1780s and, as such, his (rather than, say, the anti-Federalists') vision was mostly enunciated in the resulting federal Constitution.[b]

In these critical aspects—maladies and remedies—both Madison and De Tocqueville reflected very different perspectives of democracy and its governing institutions, all imbedded deeply in their fundamental perceptions of human nature and its all-too-dependable vulnerabilities. Let us now turn to a closer examination of their respective political statements and how they manifested themselves in the ebb and flow of American democratic theory and practice since then.

Madisonian Democracy

James Madison is widely respected as one of the giants of post-Revolutionary America, serving in the Virginia legislature, a charter member of the U.S. House of Representatives, secretary of state, and ultimately following his lifelong Virginian friend Thomas Jefferson to the presidency in 1808.[13] Assuredly, his greatest contribution to

---

[a] It is, of course, a great irony that while Rousseau was setting the *Social Contract* in Geneva, Geneva itself was refusing to let the book be sold within its city limits.

[b] Whether the fact that Madison was an active participant in the Constitutional Convention and ratification debate while deTocqueville was merely an interested and subsequent observer tinged their respective visions is an interesting question, one we cannot adequately address here.

the nation was as a member of the Philadelphia Constitutional Convention, as a spirited spokesperson and rapporteur. He was to gain even greater fame from future generations, however, as the principal author (with Alexander Hamilton and, to a lesser degree, John Jay) of *The Federalist Papers,* which have generally been credited with providing the intellectual touchstone for the states' ratification of the fledgling Constitution.[14]

Drawing upon his extensive schooling in political systems past and present, Madison represented the viewpoint that the "republican democracy" as proposed had one fatal flaw. As Madison articulated to the constitutional meetings and later in *The Federalist Papers,* he made it clear that the political faction was the predominant threat to the newly incubated democracy because of its inherently disruptive nature. The 10th *Federalist* could not be more patent in that regard, with Madison stating boldly in its very first sentence:

> Among the numerous advantages promised by a well-constructed Union, none deserves to be more accurately developed than its tendency to break and control the violence of factions. (10, p. 77)

Madison's primary concern was that political factions were a genuine threat to democracy, for they particularly portended (or intimated) the ability of a majority faction to dictate in an authoritarian manner to its minority kin; in other words, factions seeking their own gratifications could imperil the protection of minority rights and thereby undermine the democratic ethos, just as surely as the autocratic monarch. Or, when overruled or outvoted, they might well entrench an ongoing and destructive feud. (Witness the bitter animosities held by the Deep South prior to the Civil War toward the North in general and toward blacks in particular after the Civil War.) As Madison wrote,

> . . . to secure the public good and private rights against the danger of such a faction, and at the same time to preserve the spirit and form of popular government, is then the great object to which our inquiries are directed. Let me add that it is the great desideratum by which alone this form of government can be rescued from the opprobrium under which it has so long labored and be recommended to the esteem and adoption of mankind. (10, p. 80–81)

There were, Madison elaborated, two ways for effectively "curbing the mischief of factions" within a government—"the one, by removing its causes; the other, by controlling its effects" (10, p. 78). The traditional democratic theorists, such as Rousseau (and later, as we shall see, De Tocqueville) might argue for a cure predicated upon the individual and civic virtues, that is, addressing the underlying source of conflict within the citizen, one that Madison held might later surface in the aggregate as an example of his dreaded factional disputes. Madison, however, held little stock with that approach; as he explained in the 10th *Federalist*, political factions loomed ominously above the individual's civic virtue and were much more than topical or evanescent in nature:

> The latent causes of factions are sown into the nature of man. . . . A zeal for different opinions [has] divided mankind into parties, inflamed them with mutual animosity, and rendered them much more disposed to vex and oppress each other than to cooperate for their common good. (10, p. 79)

Factions, he held, were simply too much a part of man's inherent nature—the rewards were too enticing—to be alleviated by personal restraint civic virtue. As Madison elaborated in his famous angelic explanation from the 51st *Federalist:*

> If men were angels, no government would be necessary. If angels were to govern men, neither external or internal controls of government would be necessary. In framing a government which is to be administered by men over men, the great difficulty lies in this: You must first enable the government to control the governed; and in the next place oblige it to control itself. A dependence on the people is, no doubt, the primary control on the government; but experience has taught mankind the necessity of auxiliary precautions. (51, p. 322)

Or, again, in the 10th *Federalist,* in which Madison stressed that "The inference to which we are brought is that the *causes* of factions cannot be removed and that relief is only to be sought in the means of controlling its *effects*" (10, p. 80, Madison's emphases).

To confront this too-human frailty, Madison elected to "disenfranchise" the individual by replacing Montesquieu's direct and distrusted citizen participation ("democracy") with a representative or indirect democracy (Madison's "republic").[15] The first, Madison explained, was "a society consisting of a small number of citizens, who assemble and administer the government in person," and the latter was "a government in which the scheme of representation takes place . . . and promises the cure for which we are seeking." Emphasizing the distinction in terms of representation, he continued:

> The two great points of difference between a democracy and a republic are: first, the delegation of the government, in the latter, to a small number of citizens elected by the rest; secondly, the greater number of citizens and great sphere of country over which the latter may be extended. (10, p. 82)

In so doing, he consciously reduced the role of the individual citizens (including Jefferson's much-admired gentleman farmer) in political life, replacing them with a more representative and centralized albeit carefully bounded form of government. While the size of the polity was indeed a prominent criterion, the danger of destablizing, ultimately debilitating factions was Madison's principal concern. Madison expounded on the nature and benefit of deliberative bodies in the 55th *Federalist Paper:*

> . . . a certain number [of participants] at least seems to be necessary to secure the benefits of free consultation and discussion, and to guard against too easy a combination for improper purposes; as, on the other hand, the number ought at most to be kept within a certain limit, in order to avoid the confusion and intemperance of a multitude. In all very numerous assemblies, of whatever characters composed, passion never fails to wrest the scepter from reason. Had every Athenian citizen been a Socrates, every Athenian assembly would still have been a mob. (55, p. 342)

Madison's Virginian autocracy began to assert itself in this republican form of government: "the effect . . . is . . . to refine and enlarge the public views by passing them through the medium of a chosen body of citizens, whose wisdom may best discern the true interest of their country. . . ." (10, p. 82). In turn, the at-large elected representatives would collectively form opposing factions that would buffer or negate (either singularly or collegially) any given faction's move toward potential tyranny. As Richard W. Krouse observed with some irony, "Far from being a social vice, political fragmentation has now become *the* republican virtue."[16] One of Madison's numerous letters to Thomas Jefferson (the then-American ambassador to France) elaborated: "*Divide et impera,* the reprobated axiom of tyranny, is under certain qualifications, the only policy by which a republic can be administered on just principles."[17] In other words, the legitimation of (what we would later call) splinter or interest groups would presumably guard against the threatened oligarchy of the well-placed and powerful few.

More pointedly, in Krouse's view, Madison's semantic transition is particularly telling, for it sets out rather clearly his view of a viable democratic (read: republican) system:

> By implication, democracy (now always direct) becomes the corrupt and vitiated form of popular rule; republicanism (now always representative), its good or lawful counterpart. Employing this distinction, Madison argues that democracy is intrinsically incapable of alleviating the mischiefs of faction.[18]

Institutionally, Madison operationally reinforced his distrust of factions by proposing the distinct separation of powers among the three branches of government. They were deliberately designed as all equal and none controlling, a "political order" wrote Charles W. Anderson, "in which diverse factions, interests, and power-seekers would be held in stalemate, an equilibrium in which none could dominate, so that all must, in the end, deliberate the common good."[19] Madison explained himself quite eloquently in the 47th *Federalist Paper:*

> The accumulation of all powers, legislative, executive, and judiciary, in the same hands, whether of one, a few, or many, and whether hereditary, self-appointed, or elective, may justly be pronounced the very definition of tyranny. (47, p. 300)

And the 51st *Federalist,* in which he addresses the issue of how to maintain the democratic tension or balance in the state as an interaction between the three branches of government:

> To what expedient . . . shall we finally resort, for maintaining in practice the necessary partition of power among the several departments laid down by the Constitution? The only answer . . . is that as all these exterior provisions are found to be inadequate the defect must be supplied, by so contriving the interior structure of the government as that its several constituent parts may . . . be the means of keeping each other in their proper place. (51, p. 321)

By these measures, Madison proposed to protect the nascent republic from the feuding factions he feared would destroy personal freedoms and, perhaps just as important to a landed Virginian, property rights. He was, by constitutional design, safeguarding the new nation from internecine factions and disaggregating the locus of potential powers by setting them in explicit opposition. He concluded: "And happily for the *republican cause,* the practical sphere may be carried to a very great extent by a judicious modification and mixture of the *federal principle*" (51, p. 325; Madison's emphases).

The reason behind Madison's constitutional manipulation—of separation of powers and republican representative government— was that, at heart, he did not trust the individual citizen to understand the requirements of government and to govern in a dispassionate manner, to overcome the "factious spirit [that] has tainted our public administration" (10, p. 78). Madison, as a representative son of the Enlightenment, worried seriously about the irrationality and lack of constancy of the individual citizen in carrying out the Constitution's charge. Man's vulnerabilities (either individually or in factions) were, in Madison's view, too prone to be led passionately astray, leaving the government, its processes, and its very existence at great risk. So the spirit of the Enlightenment would have it. The 49th *Federalist* either revealed Madison as a cynic (if one is skeptical) or (more generously) explained his political misanthropy:

> ... there appears to be insuperable objections against the proposed recurrence to the people, as a provision in all cases for keeping the several departments of power within their constitutional limits. . . . [T]he most rational government will not find it a superfluous advantage to have the prejudices on the community on its side. The danger of disturbing the public tranquillity by interesting too strongly the public passion is a still more serious objection against frequent reference of constitutional questions to the decisions of the whole society.

> But the great objection of all is that the decisions would probably result from such appeals would not answer the purpose of maintaining the constitutional equilibrium of the government. . . . The *passions,* therefore, not the *reason,* of the public would sit in judgment. But it is the reason, alone, that ought to control and regulate the government. The passions ought to be controlled and regulated by the government. (49, pp. 314, 315, and 317; Madison's emphases)

Or, as in the 63rd *Federalist,* when he explained the importance of a Senate-like body in a carefully moderated statement and where his own preference resided:

> [T]he necessity of a well-constructed Senate . . . may sometimes be necessary as a defense to the people against their own temporary

errors and delusions. As the cool and deliberate sense of the community ought, in all governments, and actually will, in all free governments, ultimately prevail over the views of its rulers; so there
are particular moments in public affairs when the people, stimu-
lated by some irregular passion, or some illicit advantage, or misled by the artful misrepresentation of interested men, may call for
measures which they themselves will afterwards be the most ready
to lament and condemn. In these critical moments, how salutary
will be the interference of some temperate and respectable body of
citizens, in order to check the misguided career . . . until reason,
justice and truth can regain their authority over the public mind.
(63, p. 384)

In short, Madison's brief for the new nation was more republican than democratic in tone. It indicated a serious questioning of
the citizen's ability, even right (note Madison's use of "ought" in this
quotation) to govern. Rather than turn the government over to an
unstructured, passion-prone democracy, Madison—and, by extension, the Constitutional Convention—chose to disenfranchise the
citizen by a series of carefully designed checks and balances, as well
as by a representative government that effectively tempered the individual and his "misled" enthusiasms. By so doing, Madison found
himself on the horns of the democratic dilemma; borrowing coauthor
Alexander Hamilton's phraseology, Madison was forced to make a
harsh choice: "Give all power to the many, they will oppress the few.
Give all power to the few, they will oppress the many."[20] Caught between the republican rock and the democratic hard place, Madison
was forced to choose the former, but with a series of reservations and
caveats, which, in operation, ultimately gave the symbolic appearance of a watered-down, constitutional version of the latter. The only
significant drawback to Madison's carefully forged resolution of
Hamilton's posed dilemma was one that ultimately affects all modern democracies—who is the ruler and who is the ruled?

De Tocqueville and American Democracy

The count Alexis De Tocqueville came to America in May 1831
and departed the following February, thus residing and traveling in
the United States for about nine months, well after Madison had re-
tired from public life. Although De Tocqueville had certainly read and
appreciated *The Federalist Papers,* he unquestionably saw a significantly different United States than had Madison. De Tocqueville's

Democracy in America (the first volume published in English in 1835, the second in 1840) reflected upon a vibrantly emergent American culture and polity, one whose politics were on the brink of the transition from the practiced gentility of the Virginian aristocracy to the rambunctiousness of Jacksonian pluralism.[21] More critically, the context and purpose of American democracy itself had changed. As Richard D. Heffner observes in his editor's introduction to De Tocqueville's volumes,

> Thus it was not until Jackson's time that equalitarianism became the over-riding theme of American life, with majority rule its most convenient rule of thumb. . . . The notion that "to the victor belongs the spoils" was the most forthright expression of this simple democratic instinct for replacing office holders whose party had been repudiated with those who were more clearly "the people's choice."[22]

As we just noted, Madison and De Tocqueville had both shared a generalized fear of an autocratic government and proposed ways in which the United States could avoid that fate. But by the 1830s, De Tocqueville's principal concern was focused on other, more internal worries of possible despotism, such as (if we can use his chapter headings) the "Unlimited Power of the Majority . . . and Its Consequences" and the "Tyranny of the Majority" rather than Madison's earlier admonishments surrounding the potential of conflicting political factions.[23] In short, as Marvin Zetterbaum wrote, De Tocqueville "underscored his fear that democracy as most men understood it—namely, participation by the many in the act of sovereignty—was compatible with tyranny as well as with liberty."[24]

The principal difference between the two highly politic observers lay in their remedies for such threats. Whereas Madison feared political divisions and their possible tendency to overwhelm a minority and, therefore, fashioned institutional safeguards against them, De Tocqueville's democratic relief was much different. He saw democracy in a more egalitarian perspective, that is, as a function of individual "sameness," a political system for individuals primarily demanding individual responsibility as the price for personal liberties. Hence, he relied more than Madison on addressing the root cause (remember Madison perceived factions as a fundamental product of individual shortcomings but chose to confront the former[c]),

---

[c] As Madison warned in his 10th *Federalist*, "we well know that neither moral nor religious motives can be relied on as an adequate control" (10, p. 81).

prescribing personal virtue as manifested in the political arena. As Krouse was to comment, "Classical democratic republicans such as Montesquieu and Rousseau had sought to cope with political faction not by controlling its effects but, through social homogeneity and moral consensus, by *removing its causes*."[25] This distinction and the manner in which they effected their safeguards marks one of the great and enduring divisions in American democratic thought.[26]

The pivotal distinction between the two camps is how De Tocqueville viewed the *social* effects of democracy. Basically, Krouse claims that De Tocqueville viewed the democratic society as a highly individualistic political system, one differentiated by equality and characterized by an independence of thought, livelihood, and purpose; in Krouse's words, De Tocqueville saw democracy as a political doctrine that "atomizes as it equalizes, sanctifying individual reason as the sole basis of opinion and belief and concentrating thought and action upon narrowly self-centered personal ends."[27] De Tocqueville is quite clear regarding this by-product of democracy, or what later sociologists would raise as a specter of social "anomie":

> Not only does a democracy make every man forget his ancestors, but it hides his descendants and separates his contemporaries from him; it throws him back forever upon himself alone and threatens in the end to confine him entirely within the solitude of his own heart. (2, p. 194)

He is equally clear concerning the insular nature of living independent of, and largely removed from, one's neighbors and or the local socialization processes, a social behavior especially germane to an observer well-feathered in the aerie of French nobility:

> I have already observed that in democracies no such thing as a regular code of good breeding can be laid down. . . . Thus it may be said . . . that the effect of democracy is not exactly to give men any particular manners, but to prevent them from having manners at all. (2, p. 250)

The bedrock of this democratic individualism was less one of social isolation than the existence of political equality. The very first sentence of *Democracy in America* attests to that state: "Amongst the novel objects that attracted my attention, . . . nothing struck me more forcibly than the general equality of conditions among the people" (1, p. 26). It would appear that De Tocqueville's central question, then, was how to coalesce and maintain a nation whose citizens were, in equal part, die-hard equalitarians and individuals, that is, how to compose governments of free-standing individuals rather than of competing factions.

These perceived trappings of equality were the focus of De Tocqueville's attention regarding American democracy. But, by the same token, they were the genesis of what he viewed to be the cornerstone of the American political ethos, a pervasive participatory political system, one freely entered into as part of a civic responsibility. As Dahl was later to observe, "A collection of people who accept the principle of majority decision making thereby signify their willingness to treat one another as political equals."[28] The political die was far from cast: De Tocqueville himself cautioned,

> it is easier to establish an absolute and despotic government amongst a people in which the conditions of society are equal, than amongst any other; and . . . if such a government were once established amongst such a people, it would not only oppress men, but would eventually strip each of them of the highest qualities of humanity. (2, p. 306)

The same egalitarian vision, however—if it were able to resist this "democratic" version of "despotic government"—was more liable to result in De Tocqueville's fondest vision of American democracy:

> Democracy does not give the people the most skilful government, but it produces what the ablest governments are frequently unable to create; namely, an all-pervading and restless activity, a superabundant force, and an energy which is inseparable from it, and which may, however unfavorable circumstances may be, produce wonders. (1, p. 110)

De Tocqueville could hardly ignore the potential dangers of this situation, particularly the threat of a tyranny by the majority, which, given the strength of the government could readily be as dangerous as an autocratic tyranny. He clearly acknowledged that individuals might be too busy or even too unconcerned to worry about the social and political responsibilities of being free, and thus lapse unwittingly into an autocratic despotism:

> There is no need to drag their rights away from citizens of this type; they themselves voluntarily let them go. They find it a tiresome inconvenience to exercise political rights which distract them from industry. When required to elect representatives, to support authority by personal service, or to discuss public business together, they find they have not time. (2, p. 207)

De Tocqueville, however, was more optimistic than Montesquieu or Rousseau (and clearly Madison) in his response to these possible shortcomings in man's political nature. He saw American democracy as avoiding this dehumanized potential through a more participatory political life, especially as practiced through direct citizen involvement in voluntary political and social (or what De Tocqueville called "civil") organizations. He commented, "Nothing, in my opinion, is more deserving of our attention than the intellectual and moral associations of America" (2, p. 201) and continued to elaborate:

> In no country in the world has the principle of association been more successfully used, or applied to a greater multitude of objects than in America. . . . In the United States, associations are established to promote the public safety, commerce, industry, morality, and religion. There is no end which the human will despair of attaining through the combined power of individuals united into a society. (1, p. 95)

In De Tocqueville's scheme, if citizens "never acquired the habit of forming associations in ordinary life, civilization itself would be endangered" (2, p. 199). These voluntary associations were functionally designed to create intermediary layers of government (akin to Montesquieu's aristocratic intermediary bodies) but with a distinctly democratic overlay in regards to citizen participation, hence, legitimacy and authority. These "layers" were institutionalized through a series of local (i.e., decentralized) government bodies. New England town meetings were De Tocqueville's exemplars—serving as a sharp repudiation of Madison's centralized "leviathan"—and extrapolated to the national (or, again using De Tocqueville's phrase, a confederal) level:

> It is indeed uncontestable that in the United States the taste for and practice in republican government were born in the townships and provincial assemblies. . . . It is that same republican spirit, those same mores and habits of liberty, which, having come to birth and grown in the various states, are then applied without any trouble in the nation as a whole. (1, p. 166)

A critical component of De Tocqueville's vision of democracy (from Montesquieu) is the ongoing process of practical political education, intended to reveal and reward the individual's participation in the polity and to develop the requisite public spirit.[29] The introduction to political life might admittedly not be straightforward but it was essential in order to inculcate the necessary democratic values and mannerisms into its workaday citizens. In De Tocqueville's rather famous analogy,

> It is difficult to force a man out of himself and get him to take an interest in the affairs of the whole state, for he has little understanding of the way in which the fate of the state can influence his own lot. But if it is a question of taking a road past his property, he sees at once that this small public matter has a bearing on his greatest private interests, and there is no need to point out to him the close connection between his private profit and the public interest. (2, p. 196)

Thus, civic associations become De Tocqueville's ground swell for political education. He contended that "It is by taking a share in legislation that the American learns to know the law; it is by governing that he becomes educated about the formalities of government" (1, p. 318). More to the point of politics through cooperation, De Tocqueville wrote, "As soon as a man begins to treat of public affairs in public, he begins to perceive that he is not so independent of his fellow-men as he had first imagined and, that, in order to obtain their support, he must often lend them his cooperation" (2, p. 195).[d] Social democracy, he averred, begets political democracy, and vice versa, or, in John Dewey's latter-day words, "The cure for the ailments of democracy is more democracy."[30] Alternatively, one can surmise that De Tocqueville treated the right of association as the central freedom of, a driving force behind a democratic, practicing republic. Krouse neatly summarizes: De Tocqueville's "Republican political education consists primarily of the *praxis* of citizenship."[31]

The vehicle for this involvement, as just implied, was local government, which he viewed in its New England setting, proclaiming that "The existence of the townships of New England is, in general, a happy one" (1, p. 61). De Tocqueville continued to stress that

> The native of New England is attached to his township because it is independent and free; this cooperation in its affairs insures his attachment to its interest; the well-being it affords him secures his affection; and its welfare is the aim of his ambition and of his future exertions. He takes a part in every occurrence in the place; he practices the art of government in the small sphere within his

---

[d] Compare this with De Tocqueville's claim of democracy as an isolating condition (p. 25, this chapter), an apparent contradiction in the benefits of democratic rule.

reach; he accustoms himself to those forms without which liberty can only advance by revolution; he imbibes their spirit; he acquires a taste for order; ... (1, p. 61)

The township's governance provided its citizens with the practice, confidence, and the wherewithal to engage themselves in political matters, at first with local and then later, as a matter of course, with state and national responsibilities. As De Tocqueville argues,

> —how happens it that every one takes as zealous an interest in the affairs of this township, his country, and the whole State, as if they were his own? It is because every one, in his sphere, takes an active part in the government of society. The lower orders in the United States understand the influence exercised by the general prosperity upon their own welfare; ... The citizen looks upon the fortune of the public as his own, and he labors for the good of the State, not merely from a sense of pride or duty, but from what I venture to term cupidity. (1, p. 104)

De Tocqueville looks upon this experience as one of political education ("Town meetings are to liberty what primary schools are to science") to prepare citizens for their responsibilities as citizens. Even though John Stuart Mill disagreed with his French colleague in many aspects, he found particular value in this emphasis. In his preface to the English language edition of De Tocqueville's first volume, Mill writes:

> There has been much said of late—and truly not a word too much—on the necessity, now that the people are acquiring power, of giving them education, meaning school instruction, to qualify them for its exercise. The importance of school instruction is doubtless great; but it should also be recollected, that what really constitutes education is the formation of habits; and as we do not learn to read or write, to ride or swim, by being merely told how to do it, but by doing it, so it is only by practicing popular government on a limited scale, that the people will ever learn how to exercise it on a large.[32]

Or, in Mill's introduction to De Tocqueville's second volume: "A political act, to be done only once in a few years, and for which nothing in the daily habits of the citizen prepares him, leaves his intellect and his moral disposition very much as it found them."[33] Again, De Tocqueville's purpose behind these repeated political "educations" was to prepare individual citizens to assume their roles in the political affairs of the municipality, state, and ultimately nation.

De Tocqueville undoubtedly posed a much more participatory (i.e., direct) democracy than Madison's "republican" control of factions via pluralism; as Krouse (following Dewey) depicts De Tocqueville, "the only cure for the ills of social democracy . . . is more political democracy. . . . It is first and foremost a process of political education generating the intelligence and public spirit, the *moeurs,* necessary to sustain a republican polity. . . ."[34] According to Zetterbaum, De Tocqueville turned Madison's issue of warring interests on its political ear by making a virtue of a human fragility: "Out of an enlightened regard for one's own material welfare, and the intelligent pursuit of it, a good other than an economic one emerges: patriotism or public-spiritedness."[35] It also directly addresses the central question of political plausibility and practicality, for as Dahl observes with typical insight and balance: "if as a result of social indoctrination one feels anxieties in situations of political inequality; and if popular [deTocquevillian] democracy relieves these anxieties and does not create others of equal or greater severity, . . . then it would be rational to prefer populistic democracy to Madisonian democracy. . . ."[36] Elsewhere Dahl writes with emphases:

> If you believe, as I do, that *on the whole ordinary people are more competent than anyone else to decide when and how much they shall intervene on decisions they feel are important to them,* then you will surely opt for political equality and democracy.[37]

In brief, Madison chose to redress what he viewed as democracy's shortcomings through external means (e.g., an institutional balance and separation of powers) while, by contrast, De Tocqueville opted for internal (individual civic virtues through personal associations) checks and controls. The American Constitutional Convention deliberately favored one over the other. As Mark Landy has commented, "The [U.S.] Constitution is virtually silent on the obligations of citizenship. This is not accidental. It reflects the Framers' [i.e., Madison's] preoccupation with curbing the excesses of popular democracy."[38] Sandel affirms Landy's position: "The republican [Sandel's version] conception of freedom . . . requires a formative politics, a politics that cultivates in citizens the qualities of character self-government requires."[39] While De Tocqueville is left with the rejoinder that dissenting participatory democrats have voiced ever since, namely that a responsible citizenship relies primarily upon the driving assumption that "The theory of equality is . . . applied to the intellect of men; . . ." (1, p. 112), and the political consequences that necessarily apply, it has traditionally been a minority view among American political philosophers.

Visions of Democracy in Twentieth-Century America

In historical perspective, American democracy as seen from the vantage point of the twentieth century seems to have split the difference between the two political theorists, drawing upon Madison's exhortation of a governing republic with balancing factions and indirect democracy while often encouraging De Tocqueville's populist initiatives and greater citizen participation. Even though one can readily discern both threads throughout the development of the Republic, the twentieth century—with its increasing social complexity, emerging socialist and Marxist political ideologies, the exponential demands upon and the resulting rise of the central government, and growth in the specialization of social and political functions—has witnessed a marked swing toward the Madisonian arc of the pendulum, regardless of whether an "imperial" Congress or executive is holding the temporary reins of power. This swing has particularly been the case since the politics and policies of Franklin Roosevelt's New Deal with a clear continuation into Lyndon Johnson's New Republic; Presidents Ronald Reagan and George Bush, although voicing decentralization sentiments and "a thousand points of light," did little to devolve the powers of the federal government. Even today, in the face of President Clinton's State of the Union declaration that we live in an "era in which big government is dead" rhetoric and a concomitant flow of political capital for all intents and purposes being funneled back toward the (occasionally reluctant) states, no mainstream politician nor political movement is advocating a more direct, that is, participatory democracy.[e]

Perhaps the critical component consistently favoring Madison's vision of representation is simply one of magnitude, that is, the size of the potential voting population.[40] Madison himself argued in favor of a large voting population as a means of protecting the nation against factions; the larger, more diverse the voting body, he held, the less likely it would be for a specific faction to gain power. The issue of magnitude was at least partially responsible for his favoring representative government; even though he too was well aware of the New England township meetings, he foresaw that the nation's population would soon be too numerous to conduct such meetings with

---

[e] Even though Ross Perot has repeatedly advocated "electronic" town meetings, this reform is taken to be little more than a political ploy, for few have ventured the necessary policy designs and implementation plans.

any decorum, let alone resolution.*ᶠ* De Tocqueville himself saw in the full fervor of Jacksonian democracy the growth of population as an obstacle but still advocated the primacy of the individual actions of local government, principally as a means of educating and involving the individual citizen. His model of an *con*federal democracy—of social, hence political power residing in the localities and states—was his means for dealing with the magnitude of the emerging size and tendency of government manifested by Jackson's presidency and of its "to the victors belongs the spoils" characteristics.

There have been, of course, a number of political crises (indeed, a horrific Civil War) since De Tocqueville wrote his volumes. Even with the seemingly cyclic rise and fall of political liberalism, numerous constitutional amendments, and new government agencies with newly specified functions, the central processes of the American political system have not changed significantly since the days of Madison and the preference of the Constitutional Convention, in other words, popular representation through indirect democracy, again with size being the primary sticking point. Dahl is directly to the point on the central obstacle for direct (what he calls "primary") democracy: "severe upper limits are set on effective participation in 'democratic' decisions by the sheer number of persons involved." He suggests an upper bound of approximately six hundred participants who can engage in a modern polyarchic deliberative body.[41]

Still, there has been a resistant strain in American democratic theory that cherishes the relevance and utility of participatory democracy. The momentum underlying this agitation has been twofold. First, political observers in the United States have decried the American political condition as unresponsive to public needs or, more specifically, as being overly responsive to elite demands in lieu of popular positions.*ᵍ* Nor have these been merely the groaning of the temporarily excluded political elites. Many times during the twentieth century, large numbers of American voters have cast their November ballots for third-party presidential candidates, even those who fell beyond the ken of traditional American politics (e.g., Socialist Eugene Debs and Norman Thomas, Progressive Robert LaFollette, and even Southern conservatives like George Wallace and Strom Thurmond).

ᶠ Nor, of course, was Madison sufficiently the populist to advocate the primacy of individual rule, especially when it came to property rights.

ᵍ And in other areas (e.g., political favoritism) as well, but those are different matters for different volumes.

Most recently, Ross Perot captured a full 19 percent of the popular vote in the 1992 presidential elections, the largest percentage except for Theodore Roosevelt's Bull Moose/Progressive ticket in 1912. These ballots have been cast even in the face of a clear certainty that their voters' preferred candidates have had no opportunity for victory.

The second reason supporting direct democracy has resided in many "radical" political movements. Such groups that generally fall outside the center currents of American politics have argued explicitly for a more direct democratic system, like De Tocqueville's, if not for the general governance processes than at least for internal consumption for themselves, as a pledge of symbolic purity, one free of the taint of "typical," "outmoded," or (most often) "corrupted" American politics. This devolution of government was one of the principles behind the New Frontier's Model Cities policy. The Port Huron Proclamation (1962) made such a claim for the newly formed Students for a Democratic Society. Some feminist groups have posed similar democratic challenges to themselves.

Although there is no reason to doubt the sincerity of these parties' claims, their organizational politics have not supported the propositions, as both size (the obvious drawback when dealing with a growing social movement, resulting in a larger number of participants) and the "free rider" phenomenon (in which one party consistently refuses to carry a commensurate share, rather, allowing others to "carry the load" in their stead) conspired against them in this particular position. Samuel Huntington was later to say with some acerbity that "the surge of participatory democracy and egalitarianism gravely weakened, where it did not demolish, the likelihood that anyone in any institution could give an order to someone else and have it promptly obeyed," with Daniel Patrick Moynihan adding a dismal coda: "We may discover to our sorrow that 'participatory democracy' can mean the end of both participation and democracy."[42]

For instance, Kathy E. Ferguson argued that effective and democratic decision making within radical feminist circles required "open participation in decision making in a 'public space' where all participants have the opportunity for 'genuine involvement' in all aspects of collective life from economic decisions to decisions about child care and education."[43] In this argument, the inclination of an individual to engage in actions designed to promote her own interests rather than the collective interests of the group would be minimized.

In a very real way, the twentieth-century feminist movement was replicating De Tocquevillian nineteenth-century concepts of politics operating through open group associations. In this case, however, empirical evidence tended to undermine the ideal. In their study of the Seneca Women's Encampment for a Future of Peace and Justice (1983), Peregrine Schwarz-Shea and Debra Burrington found that "voluntarism, especially in combination with shared leadership and open, fluctuating participation, created a 'free rider' problem where the burden of the Encampment maintenance was unequally shared"; moreover, that "the cultural feminist tendencies of the radical Encampment organizers worsened the free-rider problem," because of the unanticipated discovery by the organizers that women would indeed engage in adopting the free rider condition, freely violating the central assumption that this would not be the case because "empowered" women were thought to be "naturally" cooperative.[44] The authors concluded that under the Seneca conditions,

> If community means suppression of *some* differences, then a lesson of the Encampment is the painful need to recognize the necessity of some coercion because "urging people to act heroically by no means insures that they will do so. . . ." [W]hat seems clear is that explicit formal coerion in the name of community necessity is preferable over the informal, hidden coercion of peer pressure. . . . We do not believe that it makes sense to assume, as did the Encampment organizers, that empowered individuals won't free ride.[45]

In addition to these two rather quixotic attempts to implement a more direct democracy that ended up basically undermining the concept, a more subtle impediment was implicitly arguing against the decentralization of American democracy, a phenomenon James A. Morone has ironically called the "democratic wish," one very much in keeping with both Madison and De Tocqueville (as well as many others):

> At the heart of American politics lies a dread and a yearning. The dread is notorious. Americans fear public power as a threat to liberty. Their government is weak and fragmented, designed to prevent action more easily than to produce it. The yearning is an alternative faith in direct, communal democracy. . . . A great irony propels American political development: the search for more direct democracy builds up the [centralized, more unrepresentative] bureaucracy.[46]

Drawing upon multiple examples in American history, but in particular upon the political movements of the twentieth century, Morone presents a persuasive case as to how the repeated attempts to decentralize power back to the individual or at least to local constituents have produced little more than a tantalizing "utopian image . . . the persistent democratic wish—cannot be achieved. Ultimately, 'the people' is a reification, a powerful political fiction."[47] What one finds in any number of demands for a decentralization of power—for example, the labor movements, the politics of racial movements, even contemporary health care—ultimately results in just the opposite, a greater centralization through an expanded bureaucracy created to implement, and then preserve the new popular policies.

Morone sketches out the process behind the "democratic wish," one that is basically the same for his cases: first, popular agitation begins with the political stalemate characteristic of American liberalism over specific issues (e.g., workers' movements and universal health care); in the second stage, people's inchoate complaints are aggregated and provoke a popular response, often through voluntary organizations, leading to, third, the development of new policies and often governmental organizations to design and implement the new policies; and, fourth, there is a return to the new (and now altered) political equilibrium. But the final two steps, in order to address the first two, invariably develop an entire new bureaucracy, which, by definition, is relatively removed and unresponsive to "the people." Thus, Morone concludes, "The lingering tension between democracy and public administration reflects the final irony of the American state-building process: democratic aspirations built a bureaucracy largely beyond popular control."[48] Even in periods of government cutbacks and "downsizing," government influence is not so much diminished; it is simply transferred from one level (e.g., federal) to another (state).

And yet, despite these setbacks, the vision of a direct democracy persists within the American polity and psyche in its "elusive chimerical promise: somehow, power can be taken away from the state and restored directly to the people. That ideal," warned Morone, "rooted in the crucial instant of the Revolutionary conflict, may be the most important false hope in American history."[49]

The Case for a Participatory Democracy

In spite of these obstinate hurdles, repeated disappointments, and noticeable failures, a viable and well-articulated sentiment continues to argue for a form of a more direct American democracy, in both theory and practice. Robert D. Putnam's masterful argument

that the American society has lost much of its social cohesiveness—
a loss that reflects unfavorably on its political bases—mirrors De
Tocqueville's proposition: individuals are educated for a political mi-
lieu by working together, so the continual fusillade of social conditions that isolate citizens from one another certainly undermines
the democratic cooperativeness envisioned by De Tocqueville and
John Stuart Mill. (Putnam entertains a wide range of possible dis-
ruptions—for example, the economy, women's participation in the
work force, divorce rates, even the American pastime, baseball—
and ultimately indicts the couch-potato romance of the Americans
and their televisions.[50]) In Sartori's vernacular, the distinct lack of
social democracy has undercut the possibility of political democracy,
thus forcing the political system into an indirect, representative system, one that perforce removes and distances the citizens from their
government. And, disturbingly, the system offers little alternative
for individual recourse, even as Americans grow increasingly disenchanted with what they wish to identify as "their" government, or
what Sandel rather awkwardly terms their "disenpowerment."

Although William Greider surely brings a vested perspective to
the discussion, his note in this instance resonates to the most fragile
theme of American democracy: "The consequences of democratic failure are enormous for the country, not simply because important
public matters are neglected, but because America won't work if the
civic faith is lost."[51] Similarly, Christopher Lasch complains about
the disenchantment of the elites with the democratic processes and
product.[52]

Two contemporary authors who have argued strongly for a
more direct democracy are Carole Pateman in her *Participation and
Democratic Theory* and Jane J. Mansbridge in *Beyond Adversary
Democracy.*[53] Pateman, drawing upon the writings of Rousseau,
James and son John Stuart Mill, Joseph Schumpeter, Robert Dahl,
and G. D. H. Cole, proposes, largely from Cole, the centrality of the
local workplace as a cradle of democracy, because the alternative is
that "Over the vast mechanism of modern politics the individual has
no control, not because the state is too big, but because he is given
no chance of learning the rudiments of self-government within a
smaller unit."[54] Linking Cole's proposition of the management of
the workplace and political governance, Pateman draws an obvious
conclusion:

> The important point . . . is that in Cole's view industry provided the
> all-important arena for the educative effect of participation to take
> place; for it is in industry that, outside Government, the individual

is involved to the greatest extent in relationships of superiority and subordination and the ordinary man spends a great deal of his life at work.

She continues, directly echoing De Tocqueville and John Stuart Mill, substituting the workplace as the latter-day version of the neighborhood association of friends:

The theory of participatory democracy is built around the central assertion that individuals and their institutions cannot be considered in isolation from one another; . . . for maximum participation by all people at that level socialisation, or "social training," for democracy must take place in other spheres in order that the necessary individual attitudes and psychological qualities can be developed. *This development takes place through the process of participation itself.* The major function of participation in the theory of participatory democracy is therefore an educative one, educative in the widest sense, including both the psychological aspect and the gaining of practice in democratic skills and procedures.[55]

Pateman's case weakens somewhat when the reader asks that she address the empirical evidence of a "democratic spillover."[h] That is, her proposition is theoretically persuasive but what evidence does she offer to substantiate her claim that democracy in the workplace (i.e., social democracy) produces a greater incidence of political democracy? Besides a case study of [formerly] Yugoslavian worker-management experiments, her most germane examples are drawn from *The Civic Culture* by Gabriel A. Almond and Sidney Verba (1965). Almond and Verba's survey of five nations did indicate that the level of political "competence" was highest in those nations (typically the United States and Great Britain) that offered the greatest number of institutional opportunities for personal participation and, moreover, they claimed that "Where local government allows participation, it may foster a sense of competence that then spreads to the national level."[56]

Certainly Almond and Verba produced path-breaking research, but this particular finding is hardly the concrete support Pateman needs to cement the crucial "spill-over" assumption necessary to tie the workplace to the governing place. Nor have the traditional venues of public administration and, more recently, public management—

---

[h]Note the close parallel with John Dewey's statement that "The cure for the ailments of democracy is more democracy."

which has a clear proprietary claim to this proposition—produced much bullet-proof evidence to that effect. Indeed, in the end, Pateman seemingly admits as much by offering her most watered-down version of the worth of a participatory political system: ". . . participation in the alternative areas [e.g., the workplace] would enable the individual better to appreciate the connection between the public and private spheres."[57] No doubt "appreciation" is a vital feature of any democracy, but one needs to wonder if the entire political system (both public and private components) warrants an upheaval simply for the sake of a more universal recognition of the "connection" between the two spheres.

Jane Mansbridge's *Beyond Adversary Democracy* poses an alternative model to Pateman's, a democracy couched largely in terms of "friendship," which is discussed in Aristotle's *Nicomachean Ethics*, where "Friendship is equality." Mansbridge contrasts a participatory democracy (which she labels "unitary") based on an agreed consensus against a representative, competitive model ("adversary") based upon the mechanism of majority rules. Thus, she sets out to "persuade cynical readers that, despite the drawbacks of the participatory democracies of the late 1960s and early 1970s, these relatively unitary institutions filled human needs that adversary institutions cannot fill."[58]

Mansbridge emphasizes the observation that modern American democracy is distinguished by its feelings of helplessness, leading to a participatory lack of interest. She quotes the sociologist C. Wright Mills in 1956 as he described the American voters: "They feel they live in a time of big decisions; they know they are not making any."[59] Moreover, if we reconsider the rather dour surveys and authors cited in the introduction, contemporary political conditions have scarcely been characterized by notable improvements; indeed, citizens today are apparently (i.e., they feel) even more disenfranchised than when Mills was writing forty years go, as approval ratings for almost *anything* political move toward depressing lows. As Greider stresses, "If citizens sometimes behave irresponsibly in politics, it is the role assigned to them. They have lost any other way to act, any means for influencing the governing process in positive and broad-minded terms."[60]

Mansbridge's principal arguments are relatively straightforward: she bases the unitary democratic logic on consensus (and draws a careful distinction between consensus and unanimity[i]), contend-

---

[i] The principal distinction between the two is that participants need not necessarily agree with a decision in order to "go along."

ing (with Madison's ghost undoubtedly part of her intended audience) that "To people steeped in the adversary tradition, the very notion of unitary democracy usually appears naive and impractical. They assume that interests [read: factions] are always in conflict." However, she counters (this time with De Tocqueville's revenant peering over her shoulder) "that the more the members of a polity have *common interests,* the less they need to protect their interests against one another, and, consequently, the less they need equal power in order to protect those interests."

In the final accounting, Mansbridge has to admit to the effectiveness benchmark often provided by adversarial procedures, noting that even in her two carefully chosen and committed examples of unitary democracy (a New England village and a small workplace), serious conflicted conditions can occur that require the participants to "shift back and forth between unitary and adversary modes of decision making, depending on the degree to which their members' interests conflict." That is, they—and she—are forced to lay aside temporarily the procedures of unitary democracy. More seriously, Mansbridge gives little indication as to what distinguishing points or evidence will determine which procedures to use; that is, the conditions that define a debate that will be suitable for unitary (as opposed to an adversary) democracy. Finally, she is forced to concede that "face-to-face assembly lets those who have no trouble speaking in public defend their interests; it does not give the average citizen comparable protection."[61] The theory would seem more persuasive than the practice.

Like Pateman, Mansbridge neglects to define and apply an evaluative litmus test, that is to say, does her unitary democracy perform "better" in terms of making "tough" decisions or is one forced to adversarial processes when facing such troublesome choices, leaving only the "easy" ones for the unitary mode? In a hyperpluralistic America, one needs to ask if there are any "easy" ones of importance left. In this case, Mansbridge is probably correct when she observes that most Americans view unitary democracy as "naive and impractical," for American politics are visibly replete with interests that are anything but common, especially in an era where diversity of opinion is seemingly a principal public value. On the other hand, she lays an excellent foundation for a possible "contingency" theory of democracy, that is, one can choose the form of democracy as a function of which mode seems the most appropriate in the context and purpose, a concept to which we shall later return.[62]

Mansbridge fails to capitalize more completely upon a potentially more significant benefit of her unitary democracy. The sociolo-

gist James S. Coleman proposes the centrality of a common understanding, a behavioral set of tacit and explicit agreements necessary
for the stabilization of any society, or what he terms *social capital*.
Analogous to the economists' concept of "physical capital" as a prerequisite investment for increased productivity purposes, Coleman
characterizes social capital as

> defined by its function. It is not a single entity, but a variety of
> different entities having two characteristics in common: They all
> consist of some aspect of a social structure and they facilitate cer-
> tain actions of individuals who are within the structure. Like other
> forms of capital, social capital is productive, making possible the
> achievement of certain ends that would not be attainable in its
> absence . . . social capital . . . is embodied in the *relations* among
> persons.[63]

Coleman's social capital, then, is a watermark of personal trust, one
that permits a society and its members to function independently of
one another but with some tangible degree of confidence in the other
members' dependability. It represents a social position well short of
authoritarian coercion and on the cooperative side of anarchy.[64]

Social capital, according to Robert D. Putnam and to a host of
very different observers, including, of course, De Tocqueville and his
reliance on civic organizations, is hypothesized to be the missing
element in today's America. In Putnam's analysis of "The Strange Disappearance of Social Capital," he compares the steady (and disheartening) decline of American civil engagement (measured in terms of
voter turnout, newspapers read daily, social trust, and types of group
membership[65]) as a function of generations. He finds strongly analogous evidence in his decade-long study of Italian democracy, in
which he posits greater democratic tendencies largely determined
by a general reliance on hierarchical (which he calls "vertical") relationships as opposed to a more broad-based ("horizontal"), independent relationship. Putnam comments on this distinction:

> Stocks of social capital, such as trust, norms, and networks, tend to
> be self-reinforcing and cumulative. Virtuous circles result in social
> equilibria with high levels of cooperation, trust, reciprocity, civic en-
> gagement, and collective well-being. These traits define the civic
> community. Conversely, the absence of these traits in the *un*civic
> community is also self-reinforcing.[66]

And social capital—the glue that bonds a society and even a nation together—is a more detectable outcome of a participatory democracy, one that is overlooked by Pateman, only alluded to by Mansbridge, and clearly addressed by Putnam, Sandel (although in slightly different terms), and Greider. For, as Greider cautions us, "If the government cannot govern effectively, it is not because the 'people' are swarming over it with impossible demands, but because the bonds of dialogue and mutual understanding between citizens and government have become so weakened."[67]

In Summary

Over the course of a little more than two centuries of constitutional rule, the United States has consistently argued for some form of a deTocquevillian democracy but invariably, for a number of reasons just enumerated, ended up with its Madisonian conception. Major political changes (e.g., those associated with Andrew Jackson, Abraham Lincoln, and Franklin Roosevelt) always held for the rights, liberties, and (most important of all) the fundamental equality of the workaday citizen in the eyes of the government, but, as Morone points out, they inevitably settled for either a more-removed representative government and/or a larger, less-representative (and even more-removed) bureaucracy. One need only reflect of Roosevelt's veritable circus of newly created bureaucratic agencies.

The reputed decentralizing tendencies of hyperpluralism have resulted in more governmental oversight and bureaucracy to regulate its divisive effects upon the body politic, one that John W. Gardner has described as the "war of the parts against the whole."[68] As a result, Americans get more embroiled with struggles over policy implementation than with a serious debate over who should rule and how. In this condition, one finds the *New York Times* featuring front-page stories headlined "Anger and Cynicism Well Up in Voters as Hope Gives Way," with everyday citizens saying,

> I've thought of moving to another country. I'm considering Costa Rica for my wife and me. If I live another 10 years, it's going to be economically unfeasible to live in this country. These politicians think they're a law unto themselves.
>
> [A disappointed Clinton voter explains:] I had to take the bumper sticker off my car. It just reached a point where it was difficult to be supportive.

> People have been voting and voting and voting for a change and
> haven't seen a difference. There's a sense that the system is broken.

and

> If there could be a gentle revolution in this country from the voters
> who just say, "It's the old, we're mad as hell and we're not going to
> take it any more." But it's got to come from the voters. Congress isn't
> going to do it. They're not going to set term limits on themselves.
> And they're not going to restrict the amount of money they can take
> in for their campaigns.[69]

There remains a small but committed number of political observers who hold that a participatory democracy is the best way to
relinquish the mortal grip of the "power elite" (an always pejorative
group that varies according to its observer) on American politics.[70]
They hold forth that, in the now-clichéd words of the Students for a
Democratic Society, "All power to the people." The problem is that no
one has really figured out how "all the people" can rule the collec-
tivity. Take Dahl's calculation as indicative: if the mayor of New York
City (or the prime minister of Sweden; both populations are roughly
the same size) were to set aside one hour each day to meet six citizens (ten minutes apiece) and did so every day of the year, by the end
of the year the mayor (or the prime minister) would have only met
three-hundredths of 1 percent of the population of New York City (or
Sweden); increasing the allocated time per day to ten hours would
only enlarge those citizens allowed to speak their respective piece
to three-tenths of 1 percent. And over the course of a four-year term,
the mayor would have met with less than 2 percent of the population, even assuming the mayor had nothing else to do but meet with
constituents. As Dahl quietly reminds us: "There are limits, mind
you, in a smaller country or a giant city. What would be an absurdity
in a small country would be grotesque in a giant one."[73]
    We can now return to Lasch's initiating question: why should
the country—that is, why should we—bother with democracy? The
issue, at heart, is one of political equality, both actual and symbolic. Dahl reminds us that political equality is "an essential means
to a just distribution of freedom and to fair opportunities for self-
development," or what the Declaration of Independence would call
"certain unalienable rights." Most public policies are predicated on
the assumption that the regulation of the nation's "social, economic,
and political structures . . . [would] achieve political equality." Yet,
since "it is easier to discover ways of reducing inequality than ways
of achieving perfect equality, . . . an advanced democratic country

would focus on the reduction of the remediable causes of gross political inequalities."[74]

At issue, then, is how the United States can reestablish a public, popular concern for its governance processes—based upon political equality—for its citizens, or, in Coleman's terms, how can it reinvest in its social capital? Participatory democracy would plausibly seem one such avenue but, in practice, it appears to be a blind alley (see Moynihan and Huntington in this chapter), leading nowhere except to more disappointments and ennui. Putnam's answers for Italian democracy—that the democratic heritage of "Palermo [Italy] may represent the future of Moscow"—are not particularly encouraging because they are as much a condition of history as current public policy. But, there is a brighter side, as Putnam more optimistically voices after De Tocqueville: "A conception of one's role and obligation as a citizen, coupled with a commitment to political equality, is the cultural cement of the civic community."[75] Or, to paraphrase Dewey's maxim, "the cure for the ailments of democracy is more civic participation."

At this point, we can turn to an examination of the policy sciences, to ask if there might be a potential key that may unlock this particular democratic riddle.

3

DEMOCRATIC FOUNDATIONS
OF THE POLICY SCIENCES

Democracy is the theory that the common people know what
they want, and deserve to get it good and hard.

—H. L. Mencken, *Little Book in C* (1916)

Introduction

According to most observers, Harold D. Lasswell was the origi-
nator of the systematic intellectual endeavor that came to be known
as the "policy sciences," although, of course, policymakers have been
given informal advice since the snake whispered into Eve's ear. In
its earliest articulation, he drew directly upon the heritage of the
American pragmatist philosopher John Dewey and Lasswell's University of Chicago mentor, Charles Merriam,[1] to define what he was to
call the "policy sciences of democracy." First broached publicly in
1949 in his *Power and Personality*,[2] the intellectual formulation was
designed to offer political decision-makers a markedly higher standard of information upon which to base their policies and programs.
One of Lasswell's doctoral students at Yale University, Ronald Brunner, has noted that the genesis of the policy sciences approach was
to "accept resources from society as a whole on the promise that such
resources will be used, in good faith, to improve policy decisions
through scientific inquiry."[3] This charter specifically provides more
systematic intelligence to improve the quality of governance in terms
of both the policy-making process and the resulting end products.

The policy sciences were consciously intended to focus on vital issues in the political environment; in Lasswell's words, "The Policy [Sciences] approach does not imply that energy is to be dissipated on a miscellany of merely topical issues, but rather that fundamental and often neglected problems which arise in the adjustment of man in society are to be dealt with."[4] In this sense, their development was to be based on a problem (rather than on a single academic disciplinary) orientation, a multi- (as opposed to a solitary) disciplinary approach (since few social problems can be fairly viewed from a single disciplinary lens), and, pivotally in the context explored here, an explicitly normative (rather than value-neutral or value-free) procedure. Each of these stood in stark contrast to the standard academic approaches of the time.

When he and Daniel Lerner edited *The Policy Sciences* volume in 1951, Lasswell advanced an even more specific, highly normative mission for the field when he wrote that the "policy sciences of democracy . . . [were] directed towards knowledge needed to improve the practice of democracy."[5] In 1950, Lasswell raised a concurrent (and equally pressing) theme of human dignity as part of his vision. With coauthor Abraham Kaplan, he proposed that the policy sciences were designed to provide "intelligence pertinent to the integration of values realized by and embodied by interpersonal relations [such as] human dignity and the realization of human capacities."[6] These goals were almost surely established in part as a reaction to Lasswell's antipathies against the recently defeated fascist powers and their repeated affronts to human dignity and democratic values. Lasswell's observations were greatly heightened by his perception of the growing technical capabilities, influence, and the potential misuse of propaganda on the national level. (Lasswell had spent the years during World War II studying propaganda techniques and effects as a staff member of the Library of Congress.) These perceptions were reflected in the policy sciences sections found in the 1965 volume, also coedited with Lerner, *World Revolutionary Elites: Studies in Coercive Ideological Movements*.

However, since Lasswell's original pronouncements, one can legitimately inquire if these charters promoting democracy and human dignity have been fulfilled or really even honored within the policy sciences communities. More concretely for the immediate purposes, we shall inquire as to what "democracy" has come to mean for the policy sciences, both as a goal and as a process. This chapter examines the development of the normative foundations underlying the policy sciences' development as a function of democratic theory and practices over the last half century. Both avenues suggest that the policy sciences as theoretically constructed are not readily amenable to democratic—recall Carl Cohen's or even Lincoln's definitions—traditions, and procedures. Nor has Lasswell's concomitant plea for human dignity become a central (or even well-intentioned) calling card. We will emphasize that these shortfalls from the original visions are discernible on both the theoretical and applied planes.

We need also to ask generally after the approaches' accomplishments. As we have seen in the first chapter, we know that the policy sciences have not realized the early expectations ascribed by their enthusiasts. In this instance, we need to wonder if their successes or failures can likewise be tied to (or disassociated from) their democratic fundamentals. To achieve this, we divide the contemporary policy sciences into two major (although not mutually exclusive) streams originally proposed by Charles W. Anderson—the utilitarian branch (often espoused by systems analysts and economists) and the liberal rationalism branch (e.g., political scientists and lawyers' variations). The former branch, as we shall see, has been the predominate application over the last forty years, as policy research has assumed the guise of applied economics. Anderson's division compares favorably with Mark Warren's split between the political philosophies he identifies as "standard liberal democracy" and "expansive democracy," Jane J. Mansbridge's unitary versus adversary democracies, and Michael Sandel's "liberal" and "republican" models, except in their respective nomenclatures.[7]

The Utilitarian Tradition

Charles Anderson points out that the utilitarian tradition of democracy, initially derived from Jeremy Bentham's (1748–1832) writings, implies that all citizens can make their own independent, freely arrived at decisions, and the resulting opinion aggregation will, in a marketlike manner, produce balancing coalitions leading (if not always smoothly) to an equitable set of public policies. It is assumed (perhaps naively) by Bentham

> that each normal adult is naturally competent to calculate an optimum balance of personal satisfaction from among the opportunities present and the information available to that individual. It is assumed that this form of reason is regular, uniform, and universal. People can be *relied* upon to think in this way.[8]

In true Madisonian fashion, the utilitarian position would argue that the polity must be constitutionally structured for the protection of the citizen and its governance practiced on the assumption
of encouraging countervailing groups as a means of avoiding despotism,[a] just as government similarly legitimates and protects the
competitive marketplace from oppressive monopolies. The critical
component of the utilitarian approach is the protection of individual
rights from excessive governmental or other parties' interventions,
although this security may not be as automatic or continuous a process as one might imagine. Adam Smith's famous economic metaphor of the "hidden hand" economy would be translated into one having a political syntax, as perhaps group theory would have it, to
investigate and then to regulate a utilitarian world.

However, citizens involved in "maximizing" their own personal
utilities often conflict with one another as they "follow self-interest
in ways to threaten the rights and liberties of other individuals."[9]
Self-interests were thought to result in a Hobbesian *bellulm omniae
contra omnes* (war of all against all) situation and, quite likely, lead
to some level of civil unrest and a resulting need for an intervening
governmental structure. To prevent civil conflict, Anderson contends,
a political utilitarian orientation "must be organized and controlled,
subordinated to a second [i.e., non-Hobbesian] scheme of reason, *presumably vested in an elite thinking differently from the people themselves*. And that is precisely the way utilitarianism works as a policy
science."

Thus, unwittingly and probably unintendedly, the utilitarian approach resurfaces Madison's deepest autocratic dread—an unfet-
tered governmental few (political architects, if you will) impinging
upon the personal prerogatives of the many (i.e., citizens) to prevent
social conflict, always in the name of the protection of the collective.
In addition, greater social goods—especially if subject to redistribution—are preferred to greater personal goods. In Anderson's trenchant summary,

> The classic, if very peculiar, assumption of utilitarianism is that the
> only public thought that the self-interested calculators who are the
> citizens are able to entertain is that they would rather live in a

---

[a] Recall Madison's letter to Jefferson: "*Divide et impera,* the reprobated axiom of tyranny, is under certain qualifications, the only policy by which a republic can be administered on just principles."

society that offered more total satisfaction than less. . . . Hence, the governors govern well if they follow a scheme of reason that increases to total utility available to the society.[10]

There are a host of reasons why this logic might be criticized beyond simple shortcomings of human nature. For instance, Anderson observes that the individual's capability to "construct a comprehensive, exhaustive, transitive calculus of personal utility . . . apart from social influence and persuasion" is usually lacking.[11] Moreover, we need to remember that perfectly competitive markets (governed in nature by Smith's hidden hand) do not occur in the political arena nor are they maintained as a pleasant coincidence of nature; witness the aphorism, "politics make strange bedfellows." They require careful, deliberate structuring and monitoring by the polity if they are to live up to the theoretical and practical expectations in order to meet the expectations of the utilitarian goals.

However, let us assume for the sake of the theoretical argument that more munificent political reading is correct, that personal preferences aggregated into political statements can avoid conflict situations. Then one can easily see how the utilitarian interpretation of the policy sciences will, in practice, quickly distance itself from direct citizen participation, however "honorable" or trustworthy the intentions of the ruling few might be. This utilitarian orientation toward government would find that the parochial, individual citizen (especially in larger, unmonitored numbers) cannot themselves be trusted to reach an equitable estimation of the utilitarian catchword, "the greatest good for the greatest number."[b] If all opinions are valued equally, then individual decisions within the society must be subjected to a majority rule vote, a process that is bound to have some occasional short-term disadvantages—with others of longer duration. As a result, citizen disappointment could have a more enduring, perhaps an eroding effect on the utilitarian position and its policies, as some find their interests consistently ignored or outvoted.

To carry out such a democratic charter, one needs to depend on a model of constitutional or social engineering to alleviate a systemic series of disappointments which, when, taken to extremes,

---

[b] The requirements of social diversity make the utilitarian approach even more difficult to encompass, a price many are willing to incur.

might be described as a despotic rule. This model is, of course, exactly what Madison offered. Madison's republic provided the new nation with a "political order, in which diverse factions, interests, and power-seekers would be held in stalemate, an equilibrium in which none could dominate, so that all must, in the end, deliberate the common good." [12] The market simile forces political decisions to be made on a majority, one-person/one-vote basis—as Mansbridge declared, an adversarial model—for a competitive market arrangement submits to no other civil resolution. At the same time, the adversarial model contributes to democracy's discontents, for someone is necessarily always left holding the short straw. At times, when the short straw regularly ends up in the same hands, as has too often been the case for Hispanic citizens, the adversarial model can be justifiably criticized for not being truly representative, and alternative measures must be sought.

Unfortunately for the Benthamites, what is dubious in theory is even further discredited in practice. Just as markets have their shortcomings, the utilitarian democracy has its. Anderson cogently summarizes:

> The policy science of utilitarian democracy then is persistently occupied with identifying and trying to remedy inequalities of influence, organization, and power, which turns out, in any modern state, to be a crude, unsatisfying, Sisyphan labor, leading at best to patchwork reforms that never do quite set matters straight. . . . Yet, ironically, calculated interest is not a self-sufficient mode of political thought. Rather, it requires the presence of a constantly vigilant and intrusive elite, always trying to contribute remedies, always ardent in pursuit of an elusive ideal of a regime that does not, and cannot arise naturally, the regime of perfect contact, or perfect equality of voice and vote. . . . [13]

This separation between the skeptical citizen and the confident policymaker—a present-day interaction of Snow's famous two-culture condition between scientists and humanists—has been reinforced by the putatively "objective" stance claimed by many policy scientists, that is, what the philosophers of science have characterized as "positivism." A Newtonian vision of the social sciences, one resulting in a position thoroughly endorsed by the durable positivist orientation (predominant in Western European culture since at least the Age of the Enlightenment), has been the touchstone of applied social sciences in the United States for much of the twentieth century. The positivist orientation, based upon the social sciences'

adherence to the protocols of the natural sciences, requires its practitioners to remain above the partisan ("subjective") politics of the
program and moment in order to retain their advertised objectivity. Elsewise, all pretensions to *scientific* (or what is thought to pass
for unimpeachable evidence and) truth are seemingly abandoned.
John S. Dryzek has said that positivism

> in policy analysis can be characterized in terms of a belief that
> policy interventions should be based on causal laws of society and
> verified by neutral empirical observation. Any practical import
> depends on policy-manipulable variables having a place in this
> causal scheme; if they did not, the result would be social science but
> hardly policy science.[14]

In Ronald D. Brunner's admirably terse evaluation, "For most policy
analysts, positivism *is* science,"[15] and therefore unyielding in its
findings and recommendations. (We shall return to the inherent
difficulties resulting from the juxtaposition of the positivist orientation and the policy sciences later in this chapter.)

The mutually occurring and reinforcing utilitarian and positivist perspectives have been directly manifested in policy analysis
methodologies, as repeatedly demonstrated by their primus inter
pares reliance on economics (e.g., benefit-cost analysis, risk analysis
and, by extension, public choice theory) and other forms of technical
advice. The economists' presumptions (some would say arrogance)
are widespread within the policy research community, especially in
commonplace practice. Applied economics, often in a variation of mi-
croeconomic analysis, were ascribed talismanic qualities with "efficiency" being the dominant criterion in the early policy texts; for example, Edith Stokey and Richard Zeckhouser stated that "Benefit-
cost analysis is a methodology with which we pursue efficiency
and which has the effect of limiting the *vagaries* of the political
process."[16]

Milton Friedman's writing on positive economics strike a conso-
nant strain: "Differences about policy among disinterested citizens
derive predominantly from different predictions about the economic
consequences of taking action—differences that can in principle
be eliminated by the process of positive economics—rather than
from fundamental differences about which men can *ultimately only
fight*."[17] Econometric models have achieved great currency in policy
fields as disparate as national energy policy and hospital cost
containment without ever having to ask the essential (and often

conveniently ignored) research question—what did the recipient citizen or the so-called "target population" want? [18]

Many of these approaches have long since been transferred by
analysts into the fabric of government activities. The primacy of this
movement was perhaps best represented by the Executive Order is-
sued by President Ronald Reagan during the 1980s to the effect that
all new federal government regulations had to be accorded a benefit-
cost analysis prior to their promulgation. This approach thereby became a touchstone (some, like George W. Downs and Patrick D.
Larkey, would say a millstone [19]) of federal policy.[c] Even more tell-
ingly, a majority of public administration scholars have adopted efficiency criteria as their preferred indicator of "good" government.

In an increasingly crowded and complex policy world—one
in which knowledge is thought to be power and governments spend
handsomely for analysis—the mantle of technical expertise, abetted
by a burgeoning bureaucracy with its own (sometimes obscured)
agenda, stands to subvert the participatory democratic processes as
surely as expert knowledge is allowed—perhaps encouraged—to
preempt lay knowledge. Christopher Lasch's indictment of elite policy planners could hardly be more direct: "The reign of specialized
expertise—the logical result of policies that equate opportunity with
open access to 'places of higher consideration'—is the antithesis of
democracy. . . ."[20] Max Weber—himself no minor influence on the
evolution of Western bureaucracy—forecast the possible social consequences of the "expert" versus the "citizen" gap:

> The "political master" finds himself in the position of a "dilettante"
> who stands opposite the "expert," facing the trained official who
> stands within the management of administration. This holds
> whether the "master" whom the bureaucracy serves is a "people" . . .
> or a parliament. It holds whether the master is an aristocratic, col-
> legiate body . . . or a popularly elected president.[20]

This is the case even if the rationale for that knowledge is often far
less than certain.[22]

Nowadays, Madison's feared factions come to government regularly and well-armed with newly minted powers, easily symbolized
by reams of analysis largely written by anonymous analysts who

---

[c] One might legitimately wonder if President Reagan was aware of what he
was asking for, never mind what he would be getting, but that is another
discussion for another time and place.

represent, in significant measures, the rulers rather than those being ruled, that is, those who effect public policy rather than those being affected. The result is that policy sciences practitioners have enthusiastically applied the utilitarian and positivist traditions to their craft, thus permitting them to celebrate the influence of the analytic few to Madison's already-removed republic of indirect democracy. In so doing, the end result ever deepens his proposed governmental "indirectness" until one might justifiably wonder if the democratic connections were still functioning, and, if so, at what expense of representativeness, fidelity, and, ultimately, citizen confidence in the government.[23] At best, the pulse seems wan, as repeated public opinion polls have revealed.

Under the utilitarian banner, "human" factors, such as politics, social conditions, and perhaps even Lasswell's human dignity, are not commonly permitted to be included in the analytic calculation, because, as microeconomists are wont to tell us, "you can't make interpersonal utility comparisons." In spite of the pioneering work of humanists like Lasswell, Kaplan, and Robert K. Merton, most of the early policy research—the intellectual heritages underlying the present-day policy sciences—was carried out by technicians, usually systems analysts and operation researchers. Their positivist orientations pushed them in pursuit of a clearly defined objective function, leading to an equally clearly defined optimal solution set requiring little (if any) contribution from the intended recipients. These removed perspectives were subsequently augmented by economists—utilitarians to their epistemological core—who predicated their policy recommendations on supposedly "objective" economic relationships pursued by rational actors employing lifeless data, again requiring little knowledge of the projected clients' particular needs or the political climate in which public policymakers, by definition, must operate. The results were all-too-predictable: policies—sadly lacking theory—based upon data—sorely lacking validity let alone simple pertinence—that were hardly the sole basis for good policy.[24]

The reason for this less-than-democratic situation was that under the prevailing utilitarian paradigm further seconded by positivism, elite thinking *should* hold societal sway as it moved rather confidently toward the "greatest good for the greatest number." As Robert A. Dahl pointed out under the rule of comparative advantage, this delegation might make sense for a brain surgeon or a ship's captain, but not in the case of democratic governance.[25] Furthermore, this assumption of governmental power in pursuit of civic order violates the primary assumption of utilitarianism, that is, every person's opinion is weighted relatively the same and they will naturally seek their own preferred economic and political order.

Nor is this distance simply a benign artifact of theory. David T. Ellwood, for years one of the nation's leading academic specialists concerning social welfare policy, was invited by the Clinton administration to become the assistant secretary of the Department of Health and Human Services. He was charged with specific responsibilities for the welfare reform that had been a prominent part of Clinton's fall campaign platform (to recall the campaign cant, "to end welfare as we know it"). By his own admission, however, Ellwood had had little actual physical contact with the poor and their depressing mien. In July 1993, a Clinton administration speech writer (with many fewer social welfare credentials than the new assistant secretary) promised during a press conference that Ellwood would soon "go out and talk to some real people" [*sic!*].

Following a series of visits to poverty locations—a trip outside Memphis reputedly being the most disturbing—Ellwood reported back on the familiar portraits of poverty he apparently had never experienced on a firsthand basis:

> We saw a woman in a horrendous rural poverty situations. Houses with no windows. Broken down ceiling. No toilet. It was just absolute, total abject poverty.

His conclusion was remarkable for what it implied—Ellwood's "absolute, total abject" lack of workaday exposure to the very people and situations he was being asked to correct. In his words, the trip to Memphis "was a radicalizing experience, radicalizing because what we saw was really, really horrible."[26] Although none would dispute Ellwood's genuine concern for the plight of the poor, seemingly the halls of Harvard had blinded Ellwood to the miseries of Memphis, even though welfare reform was undoubtedly targeted toward the latter rather than his more familiar haunts. Thus, Ellwood and others in Clinton's welfare reform camp, however sympathetic to the plight of the destitute and impoverished, have found themselves doing social welfare recipients a real disservice, both materially and psychologically. As Helen Ingram and Anne Schneider express the situation, the "rationales policymakers used to explain why policies continue to levy costs on those who have not fared so well in the capitalist economy reinforces images of dependents and deviance" upon the unfortunate.[27]

In this instance, Ellwood and his colleagues were, in effect, acting in concert with the utilitarian tradition of the better-informed few prescribing for the less-informed but more-affected many. Sincerity was not at issue; more germane were the greatly different value structures between the groups that were often ignored or discounted. Unlike Dahl's physician or ship captain, however, the results have left much to be desired for all concerned, since social welfare continues to be a bone in the throat of the Clinton administration and a continued humiliation for many of those covered by social welfare policies, even in the face of the recent welfare reform legislation. In this case, there was none of Dahl's comparative advantage, and, even if there were, it would not reside in the expert's court, because, in such cases, personal values will override "scientific" expertise.

One possible consequence of this expert-to-citizen form of the policy sciences is that its "bottom line"—its policy results—have mostly proven to be unsatisfactory, perhaps even dismal. For a variety of reasons,[28] policy research has been methodologically rich and results poor, as its practitioners have started to express reservations toward the approach's present-day noblesse oblige. Alice M. Rivlin, speaking as the outgoing president of the Association of Policy Analysis & Management and drawing upon her years of policy research, explained to the hard core of economics-oriented analysts present: "Economists . . . in their usual fashion, have been short on realism and long on theory and prescription."[29] A 1991 review of microsimulation modeling by a National Academy of Sciences commission revealed the endemic policy shortcomings of economic modeling and computer simulations—long the intellectual soul of economic modeling activities—prompting a call for a "second revolution" in policy analysis regarding the validity of the data and model reliability; as Eric Hanushek, the commission's chair explained the commission's predicament:

> We're talking about a second revolution in policy analysis. The first was to bring about systematic analyses about costs and benefits of policy. The second we're calling for is to worry about the accuracy of the estimates and improve them.[30]

Lastly, Brunner was nothing but candid in explaining the ongoing relationship between positivism and the policy sciences, one virtually dictating a continuing cooperation in spite of their lack of beneficial results:

> Nevertheless, the game continues: Positive theory and method serve to justify another conclusion about the specific context, and

fit in the specific context serves to justify another theoretical generalization. . . . Positivism thus functions as a myth, providing a rhetorical justification of research standards based on "hard" methods and universal forms, and for the research that conforms to these standards. But the persuasive power of the rhetoric stems from the Newtonian ideal, not from the record of positive research in the behavioral sciences.[31]

Admittedly more outspoken than most, John Dryzek has asserted that the policy sciences' underlying utilitarian assumption of the "rational actor" or "economics man" model (a mode he characterizes as "instrumental rationality") renders them highly suspect in the theoretical and practical senses and inevitably inadequate to the task of recommending policies in line with the needs of the targeted clientele. Dryzek argues that the reluctance (in the case of many methodologies, the conceptual inability) of the rational actor model to consider and include political and normative implications of policy in a coherent fashion places the emphasis of merit or worth of the *approach* on the credibility of a rather restricted set of administrative procedures rather than on the openly observed *process* or final outcome. Ultimately, Dryzek continues, these analytic exercises produce more than their share of unfortunate failures for apodictic reasons, because the values that would otherwise "matter" have been largely set aside or attributed to analytic convenience or a standard assumption of programmatic efficiency; democracy, in this instance, becomes a third-order consideration. In Dryzek's brutal claim, instrumental rationality

> destroys the more congenial, spontaneous, egalitarian, and intrinsically meaningful aspects of human association . . . represses individuals . . . is ineffective when confronted with complex social problems . . . makes effective and appropriate policy analysis impossible . . . [and, most critically] is antidemocratic.[32]

James S. Fishkin refers to this failure to produce useful bilateral policy actions as due to a *"disconnection* with politics,"[33] although there is no doubt in his mind as to who is being disconnected from whom or what. Louise G. White claims that such a bifurcation makes "it more difficult for the broader public to have an influence,"[34] thereby reinforcing Greider's sour thesis; in essence, *nobody* is telling the people much about the troubles of governing. That disjoint is at the root of their distrust of government as well as, ultimately, its vision of democracy.[d] Hank C. Jenkins-Smith sums up the problems inherent in a utilitarian pursuit of the policy sciences: "Thus, an unintended side effect of policy analysis may be to erect barriers in the way of important ends of participatory democracy."[35]

In summary, the Bentham-inspired, Madison-articulated models of analysis (or what latter-day scholars refer to as the "rational" school), reinforced by the trappings of positivism, have assumed the predominant brunt of the policy sciences' traditional practice and orientation revolving around institutional measures and technical expertise. The vast majority of policy analysts has therefore left the De Tocquevillian or participatory branch of American democratic theory relatively untouched as they migrate toward the utilitarian tent, seeking the convenience and prestige that defends and utilizes their technical expertise over lay opinion.[36] To the point, Mark Warren concludes, it "holds, in effect, that it is desirable to depoliticize as many spheres of society as possible, rather than to democratize them,"[37] as a means of continuing the status quo.

Even though much of the domestic American politics of the twentieth century has often been depicted as a series of moves toward a more direct democracy with the decentralization of authority and the outsourcing of responsibility (although, James Morone and others have contended that these have been failures, maybe even hollow charades), these movements have been largely a reflection of the utilitarian position. As America moves into the twenty-first century, utilitarianism (and its faith in microeconomics) rather than democracy has been shown to be the more decisive component in the post-Lasswellian policy sciences' methodologies and resulting policy recommendations.

Liberal Rationalism

An alternative to the utilitarian tradition is what Charles W. Anderson calls "liberal rationalism," which he primarily attributes to the discipline of law. Warren, a political scientist, talks of much

---

[d] One is naturally reminded here of Paul Newman's famous performance of "Cool Hand Luke," in which the recurrent theme between Luke and the prison officials was, "What we have here is a failure to communicate." These failures, of course, are typically the fault of both sides.

the same set of ideals when he refers to "expansive democracy."[38] This concept principally refers to classic or "standard" democratic liberalism, in which political activists work to ensure a more equitable redistribution of justice and social resources. The heart of this political philosophy requires a sharp denial of utilitarianism, claiming that individuals are unable to think independently toward societal goals and therefore require some sort of benign assistance to articulate what behooves a reasonable person and how he or she acts as well as what the society manages to produce. Liberal rationalism reflects the very essence of big, albeit benevolent government. Its demise has long been predicted, although only recently been mandated, as politicians of every political stripe and level now state that governments can no longer be "big," and that "bigness" itself precludes benevolence.[39]

The rhetoric of liberal rationalism purports to argue for egalitarian principles and for the protection of individual rights. As Warren notes, "These theories argue for increased participation in, and control over collective decision making, whether by means of direct democracy in small-scale settings, or through stronger linkages between citizens and institutions that operate on broader scales."[40] Michael J. Sandel criticizes liberalism for placing too few bounds on its citizenry, leaving them largely rudderless and feeling disenfranchised.[41] Its cumbersome, everyday practice requires that the public weal ultimately be delegated to others as a means toward resolving the often complex and inevitably protracted governmental processes. In fact, liberal rationalism demands lucid thinking and rational decision making on the part of the individual as a social characteristic, for, according to Anderson, it assumes that, under its regimen, all citizens, "whatever their culture, tradition, and place in history, will recognize this necessity for reciprocal restraints, trust, and goodwill if they are thinking clearly."[42] By the same token, they will also admit to a requirement for a civil government for those occasions when these presumptions of lucidity fail.

In the final balance, comments Anderson, this recognition legitimates "those of us who can think matters all the way through and recognize the need for mutual toleration, restraint, and trust have a perfect right to use coercive public power to restrain those who will not be rational."[43] It requires a trusting citizenship, one willing to abandon those prerogatives of governance, or at least willing to acquiesce in the loss of those rights. Conversely, it delegitimates those citizens whose thought and behavior patterns are less clear-cut and thorough, because they are seen as reacting adversely and uncivilly when groups disagree, again as posited by Ingram and Schneider in terms of the subtleties of policy design.[44]

To implement these liberal assumptions, citizens must establish an intermediary and unrepresentative layer of governors and expertise, created to define and then to carry out the public's welfare in the public's stead. The ability that this group utilizes, however well-meaning and possibly even correct, again separates the governing elite from their nominal constituents, as the leaders, perforce, decide for the citizen. The examples are numerous—ranging from school boards, legislators, government regulators, and virtually whatever bureaucracy or technology one wishes to name—and sometime stand in opposition to one another. For instance, the Progressive Era was best known for a series of governmental reforms designed to return direct democracy to the people (e.g., ballot initiatives, recalls, and referenda); but it also inserted large numbers of professionals into government (e.g., city managers and regulators) whose roles simultaneously undercut the movement's democratic tendencies, apparently with the assumption that democratic citizens were unable to work their way through the underbrush of government demands in order to reach well-informed policies. How else can one explain social welfare programs that insist on the father *not* being present to assist in child rearing at the risk of losing benefits? The end product is procedurally analogous to the utilitarian democratic structure and processes in that, once more, it establishes government in which the many relinquish their rights to the ruling few. In this case, convenience might be the motivating factor but the endgame is the same.

As with the utilitarian philosophy, liberal rationalism can have a direct effect on public policy formulation. No better recent example of liberal rationalism exists than the Clinton administration's strategy to devise a national health care policy, at least partially to provide coverage for the approximately thirty-seven million Americans without health insurance. Following Clinton's November 1992 election, a committee of health care experts was convened to meet for a few months in tight secrecy under the personal direction of the president's wife, Hillary Rodham Clinton, with Ira Magaziner being appointed to provide project management. Under the guise of preserving secrecy, even the names of the participants were closely held until a civil suit was brought, claiming that names must be made public because of Mrs. Clinton's position, that is, the president's wife was the study's chair even though formally she was viewed as being outside the government.[e] Moreover, communications within the group was restricted, as staff working papers were withheld from members of the policy-making group by Magaziner's orders. It was, to quote a participant, "one of the strangest things I've ever been involved in."[45]

Under Mrs. Clinton's prodding and guidance, the group labored strenuously to produce a 1,364-page proposal on how to reform the nation's health care delivery system. Only after the plan was apparently completed did administration members pause to inquire as to its acceptability to the health care providers and to the ultimate recipients, to say nothing of the enacting Congress and of its own welter of interests and ideologies. Not entirely unexpectedly, the proposed Clinton health plan never saw the light of legislative day, dying a rather natural death in Congress, with both Republicans and Democrats disavowing the study group's research scope and recommendations. Whether or not it would have met with greater success had there been a wider range of interests represented or been completed more or less on time is anybody's guess, but that should not distract from the reality that under its defined structure, success was not in the cards.

Thus, the hubris of liberal rationalism (or perhaps the contending camps of the general model of liberalism if the bureaucracy or the Congress can be construed to have its own peculiar brands) toppled the acknowledged sequoia of President Clinton's first term. The reason was not that the American health care delivery system was not troubled by rapidly rising health costs, its exceedingly technical and complex scope, nor the presence of various contending health insurance policies (i.e., third-party payers). The primary reason was that it was also important—in fact, too important to the millions of people without medical insurance (or the underinsured)—to be absconded from the American democracy system by a study group of five hundred experts, who nobody seemed to know (and whose very identities the government had consciously decided to keep hidden).

A second place where liberal rationalism falls short is that it largely ignores the key to "expansive" democracy, that is, the possibility that people find their self-images enhanced in a democratic vein if they are permitted to practice (maybe even come to understand)

---

[e] The courts found that Mrs. Clinton held no formal government office, as the plaintiffs contended; however, her status as the president's wife—the First Lady—made her a de facto government employee, hence allowing the courts to preserve the secrecy of the panel.

democracy, leading to a greater involvement in their governance. Although this concept falls into a highly normative arena relatively untouched by empirical studies, the basic assumption is that people will consider themselves better off as a function of a preference for living in a democratic society, one in which theoretically they can openly engage in the act of governing. Warren explains that "Democracy is valuable primarily because humans value both activities that allow them to grow and develop and control over the growing and developing."

This "self-transformation" thesis that Warren proposes has a direct lineage in the American context that can be traced back to the writings of De Tocqueville, who looked upon local civic involvement and voluntary organizations as a very real form of political education toward a greater democratization. (Indeed, one can readily understand how many emigrants to the United States at least partially accepted the self-transformation argument as an essential part of their political socialization.) One can imagine De Tocqueville rather than Warren writing that "increased participation is likely to encourage substantive changes in interest in the direction of commonality, transforming conflict in the direction of consensus."[46] Or the pragmatist philosopher John Dewey, avowing that "the best cure for democracy is more democracy" in direct contrast to the institutional theories championed by Madison's philosophical descendants or liberalism's preemptive model of governance.[f]

Moreover, the democratic myth perpetrated by liberal rationalism disowns the citizen from the intrinsic values derived from democracy itself. This is the situation many Americans currently find themselves in, for they no longer appear to believe that their opinions matter in a wide range of subjects, from job security to government programs to the siting of professional sports franchises. And the aura of expertise goes out of its way to emphasize that, in fact, they do not matter because the issues of government do appear to be complex and technically daunting. There would appear to be a direct trade-off between the poles of technical or economic complexity and the democratic ethos, although a number of policy scholars like Richard Sclove and John Bridger Robinson have steadfastly denied

---

[f] For those enticed with the "who said it first" game, we should admit that Governor Al Smith of New York was quoted as saying in 1933 that "All the ills of democracy can be cured by more democracy." Whether he had previously read Dewey's *Public and Its Problems* (1927) is uncertain.

such a linkage.[47] Henry Kariel captures the essence of what is at stake:

> These personages may well know what is best for others. But the better they know, that is, the more objective and helpful they are, the more they jeopardize popular participation. . . . Those whose civic center—or library, museum or city hall—it is must help to create it, even if the policy process thereby becomes untidy and the final result more cluttered and less manageable than professional planners would hope. Economic losses may be political gains.[48]

There are a few examples in which these obstacles are being challenged, where the stakes might be perceived by citizens to be particularly high—environmental politics is one such example of the primacy of *homo civicus* over *homo economicus*[49]—or fundamentally normative in their arguments—of course legalized abortion or, by similar logic but at the other end of life, the death penalty is the great stickler here—but these are not the norm. Rather, it would seem that liberal rationalism is permitted to establish the broad boundaries of governance and then to operate with relative impunity within them. Once again, citizens ultimately find themselves disenfranchised from the democratic processes.

A Comparison

Thus, while their respective rationales might be different, the utilitarian and liberal rationalism schools both are seen from the democratic perspective as distancing the people from their government. They prescribe a dense, often obscure layer of bureaucracy and expertise well above—supposedly well beyond the ken of—direct citizen participation. These phenomena are what the present argument would advance as a direct political continuation of the Madison (as opposed to the De Tocqueville) vision of American democracy. It is not to claim that one approach or the other is an "inferior" or "wrong" brand of democracy (whatever those appellations might portend). Rather, nothing more profound is implied by that evaluation than to observe that the two visions are fundamentally different—indeed, as different as Madison and De Tocqueville themselves. Therefore, the operating rules suitable for carrying out the first one might not be suitable for the other.

More important for the American policy sciences in the context of a democratic setting is that the opportunities for policy recommendations and implementation provided by the De Tocquevillean stream have not been realistically tested or really even tried except by fringe political groups, and then not in the conventional policy analytic mode. Indeed, it is implausible to expect that they can be assessed by a policy community that adheres closely to either the utilitarian or the liberal rational model. This is a strange disciplinary boycott because other political functions are increasingly being judged on their allegiance to decentralization, a strategy inviting widespread participation, mostly by organizations but certainly not precluding individual participation.

John Dryzek has proposed that the elite orientation of the policy sciences has revealed its tendencies toward the "policy sciences of tyranny." "By tyranny," Dryzek explained, "I do not mean the authoritarian dystopia feared by Lasswell, but any elite-controlled policy process that overrules the desires and aspirations of ordinary citizens."[50] Hank C. Jenkins-Smith has reviewed much of the literature that worries over the possibility that the policy sciences of democracy might be literally transformed into the policy sciences of tyranny and comes to the conclusion that while the threat might be latent, there are "data [that] analysts are far from achieving the status of all-powerful technicians and that the likelihood of obtaining that status appears slim."[51]

However reassuring Jenkins-Smith's reasoning might be to democratic thinking, the situation is still troubling. He argues that the main reason for the policy analysts' lack of effect within governmental circles is not their deafness to the vox populi but the fact that policy decision-makers do not yet have sufficient confidence in the craft of the policy scientists to provide highly credible answers, that is, guidance. This is not to deny the possibility that the potential toward tyranny is absent—Lasswell himself coined the phrase the policy sciences of tyranny in 1949, Dryzek revisited it forty years later, and Jenkins-Smith himself was certainly cognizant of the threat[52]—only that the policy sciences have not presented themselves in such a despotic form at least partially because they are not taken as ironclad gospel by policymakers. This is hardly a blameless instance for the policy scientist desirous of policy credibility, let alone deserving the democratic ascription. Still, one must legitimately wonder about the body politic's democratic condition when critical regulations are drawn up and executed by analysts and administrators who are, simultaneously, several layers removed from elected representatives and at least that many steps removed from the effected population (to say nothing of regulators who are more closely associated with the very parties they are supposed to be regulating rather than citizens).

This condition is particularly nettlesome as new technologies and methodologies seemingly make it impossible for the layperson to become involved in policy decisions, and, likewise, for policy-makers to understand what is at stake.[g] The analysis and policy-making underlying the search for a national energy policy during the 1970s illustrates both the isolation and complexity components of the contemporary policy sciences.[53] Policy analysts are prone to defend their isolated status as designed to insulate their analysis from vested political influences but this is an empty excuse; too many analysts have already admitted in numerous ways that their activities are at heart and by necessity intrinsically political in nature. Failing to connect with the political world would render their activities as little more than academic exercises.

However, these obstacles to a lay involvement in policy research are not dictated nor enforced by immutable laws of physics; they are man-made rules and like anything man-made, can be circumscribed by other persons. For instance, Paul Bracken and Martin Shubik have carefully studied one of the most arcane, complex, and lethal technologies one can imagine—nuclear warfare.[54] For years, it was "accepted wisdom" within the Pentagon and its "in-house" civilian strategists that nuclear strategy was too difficult to share with the country, that the "wizards of Armageddon" were members of a sacred priesthood that broached no outsiders to their decision-making counsels.[55] But Bracken and Shubik made the strong normative argument that citizens should—indeed, ought to be for there can be no alternative but to—be involved in the nuclear *danse macabre*. Nuclear strategy was (and still is) a value-laden policy of the first magnitude, one that consumed large amounts of national resources (estimated at close to three *trillion* dollars) and possibly portended the destruction of civilization; many went so far as to call it immoral. Regardless, to have anything less than full citizen participation would have itself been immoral.[56] The public demonstrations of the early 1980s against nuclear weapons was a major step toward that realization,[h] "an extraordinary grass-roots, nationwide movement to stop

---

[g] Or, if Citro and Hanushek's National Academy study on miscrosimulation is to be believed, many experts as well.

[h] One needs to add that these demonstrations were bitterly opposed by then-president Reagan.

the nuclear arms race," which was later legitimized by the nuclear weapons treaties negotiated in their wake.[57]

In summary, with a few important exceptions, the quotidian policy sciences have become an elite, sequestered activity, one whose services to democracy seemingly come as an afterthought to their primary fealty to their governmental agencies. Although the policy sciences are usually a function of a utilitarian approach, we have seen that a liberal rational defense for this behavior is also applicable. Their traditional positivist methodologies as well as their putative removal from politics have increasingly distanced the policy analyst from the policy recipient for the programs under discussion, as they self-consciously recluse themselves from the hurly-burly but imperative normative aspects of politics.[58]

This democratic dilemma is not a Manichean condition; we need not be faced with a policy sciences of tyranny to admit that we are faced with a policy sciences that is less-than-democratic in the direct representation, participative sense of the word. If we are in fact dealing with the policy sciences of democracy, then it is a strained democracy, one at its most indirect and removed, in which unelected analysts and administrators are being entrusted (often by other unelected officials) to represent popular interests and necessities. Madisonian democracy faithfully filtered through Weberian bureaucracy, if you will, but, in any case, a system far short of its Lasswellian heritage and democratic ideals. Thus, the policy sciences directly lend themselves to the general popular disappointment with government, its activities, and, indirectly, democracy itself.

The policy sciences have typically chosen not to avail themselves of the opportunities occasioned by the participatory, De Tocquevillean philosophy of governance. Recent amendments to the tradition policy sciences paradigm by an expanded community of policy scientists and their new interpretations have provided alternative possibilities to overcome many of the traditional impediments to a more democratic policy sciences and particularly to a more participatory model. Therefore, let us now turn to an examination of the underlying assumptions that contribute to an alternative set of policy paradigms.

4

THE POLICY SCIENCES
FOR DEMOCRACY

Democracy is the recurrent suspicion that more than half of
the people are right more than half of the time.

—E. B. White, *The New Yorker*, 3 July 1944

Introduction

In the previous chapter, the basic argument was posed that the
policy sciences under its two main variations have been lax in addressing Harold Lasswell's mandate concerning the "policy sciences
of democracy." Rather, to many observers, they have been more at-
tune to the "policy sciences of the elite" fought between warring and
well-financed interest groups, with the main bone of methodological
contention being their degree of quantitative (i.e., what we have seen
to be an unrepresentative) analysis. Increasingly, they are predominantly being utilized to promote or defend public policy decisions concerning corporate choices (assuming that government agencies may
adopt public variations of corporate behaviors) rather than individuals' personal (even aggregated) choices, because the latter are perceived, especially by the citizens themselves (at least those who seem
to care), as being denied a credible voice.

Variations of these behaviors are found in the countless halls of
government, hidden in the nooks and crannies of almost any administrative agency, as one might have predicted, because knowledge (or
comparative knowledge in this instance) often implies bureaucratic

power, or at least a genuine presence at the public policy table. Nor does modern policy analysis play partisan favorites, as might earlier have true for liberal causes or Democratic administrations (e.g., many nonprofit organizations as well as Secretary of Defense Robert McNamara's Pentagon "whiz kids" and President Lyndon Johnson's "War on Poverty"). Frank Fischer describes how politically conservative "think tanks" (such as the American Enterprise Institute or the Cato Institute) have assumed an analytic prowess supporting conservative programs heretofore mainly ascribed to liberal counsels. Likewise, a significant growth in the number of policy research centers does not necessarily validate Lasswell's injunction of the policy sciences ensuring more democratic government through better information, for, as Fischer cautions, "the role of policy planning organizations and the reform strategy—conservative as well as liberal—raises serious questions for democratic government and their traditional understandings of the public's role in it."[1] Institutional or bureaucratic influence rather than citizens' democracy would appear to be at stake.

These nonpartisan applications of policy analysis should come as no surprise, for they manifest the "inchworm" nature of analytic politics. Henry Aaron of Washington's liberal Brookings Institution has characterized policy research as a reserved, conservative enterprise; as he advises, "research, insofar as it exercises independent influences on opinions about complex social questions, tends over time to be profoundly conservative in its impact."[2] This marginalist bias does not so much address the policy sciences approach in terms of ideological partisanship, but, in terms of potential change, an approach that favors small, piecemeal, "social engineering" changes in lieu of fundamental alterations. In other words, the policy sciences have traditionally supported politics as they are practiced and compromised rather than preached.

In keeping with the incrementalist, satisficing, or muddling through schools of thought, the policy sciences, if they were thought to be successful, were held to operate most effectively on the margins. There surely is ample cause to adhere to this maxim but, equally surely, there is good cause to realize that the shibboleth should not be held sacrosanct. Political events over the past few years have shown that quantum changes can occur in political arenas. To name two: in 1989, the annus mirabilis in international politics when communism lost its empire, and, in 1994, the coming of a Republican "Contract for America," which has not only transformed the Republican party, but the Democratic party as well. In addition, the traditional incremental nature of policy research has hardly covered itself with professional glory in the face of a number of failures due to errors in both omission and commission.[3]

For these reasons—the proliferation of the policy sciences into an arena of dueling analytical fiefdoms, often unwilling to reach resolution, and their marginal means stuck fast in mediocre measures—it is hard to believe that Lasswell's charge for the policy sciences could be honestly achieved. Remembering Lasswell's words—"The Policy [Sciences] approach does not imply that energy is to be dissipated on a miscellany of merely topical issues, but rather that fundamental and often neglected problems which arise in the adjustment of man in society are to be dealt with."[4]—makes that transition even more difficult. Without abandoning the everyday policy perspectives, one has to ask if the policy sciences in their contemporary practice are tacitly surrendering their potential capability —or even an occasional heroic intention—to effect fundamental changes.

For these reasons, I find myself persuaded by Douglas Torgerson's scintillating metaphor (drawn from Leszek Kolakowski) comparing the respective roles of the "priest and the jester in the policy sciences":

> . . . the priest is one who "sustains the cult of the final and the obvious" while the jester, in contrast, "doubts all that appears self-evident." The priest follows tradition, the jester is impertinent. The priest prizes unity, form, and closure. The jester, perhaps appearing ludicrous, is a friend of openness, paradox, and diversity. . . . Without the priest there can be no coherent focus; without the jester, no lively challenge for development.[5]

In other words, it would appear imperative that the policy sciences, like virtually every other contemporary movement, need to be open to diversity and challenge, only more so given their previously proscribed multidisciplinary roles, problem orientation, and normative goals. In this ecumenical spirit, we should occasionally be willing to exchange our cardinal's miter for the jester's coxcomb, and vice versa, although never forgetting where we have placed the other hat. For now, let me wear the coxcomb, erring on the side of the radical, with the comfortable confidence that my possible excesses will be tempered by the thoughtful reader.

This chapter, then, will examine alternative means to the traditional policy sciences' activities that are greatly colored by positivism in general and microeconomics in particular. The argument is hardly a new one; Laurence H. Tribe raised much the same criticism in 1972, barely a year after Lasswell published his *Pre-View of Policy Sciences*.[6] But, for reasons just implied, the 1990s are more propitious for a revision in the policy sciences' paradigm when their shortcomings are more apparent than they were in the 1970s (when the policy sciences were still and hopefully somewhat experimental) or the 1980s (when they were being usually and uncritically accepted).

The purpose in this chapter will be twofold. First, we would contend that the policy sciences should be made more realistic and insightful, albeit at the possible price of being somewhat less "rational." That is, the policy sciences need to reflect both the micro- and macropolitical world with greater verisimilitude and empathy, perhaps their greatest shortcomings at the present time. Second, and of equal importance, we want to move the policy sciences more positively, more definitively toward the "policy sciences of democracy." For both of these exercises, we turn to some new expositions within the more traditional policy sciences paradigm, and, as well, to two emerging movements in the social sciences, postpositivism and critical thinking.

There are, as we shall see, substantial overlaps between the latter two schools; indeed, postpositivism is the generic epistemology, with critical theory being a component. However, drawing upon the distinctive features of both is necessary to derive and support a proposed "participatory policy analysis" that should result in a more involved (in Mark Warren's words) expanded democracy in the De Tocquevillean sense of the word. One should make no mistake about the portend of these activities, because they ultimately imply a constitutional change in the policy sciences—in their everyday processes, their academic training, their end product, and, one trusts, their democratic vision.

Multidisciplinary Approaches

When I propose a revision of the present policy sciences model, I am not suggesting a zero-sum game in which the traditional "scientific" approach to policy research would be cavalierly scuttled. Rather, I am suggesting a greater catholicity—a choice dictated by the requirements of the issues-areas at hand rather than the researcher's standardized tool kit—while still retaining the necessary coherence and rigor regardless of the chosen methodology. Certainly by now there is sufficient evidence that qualitative methods such as field research, participatory action research, and even grounded theory can be just as demanding as strictly quantitative models,[7] and that one's policy research should not necessarily suffer strictly as a function of "numeracy." Following the lead of critical theory, the natural science model should be only one of many complementary modes of policy inquiry, all equally legitimated *as a function of problem under investigation*: all are necessary, none is sufficient. In this, I am in close agreement with the late Abraham Kaplan:

> Policy must be scientific to be effective. . . . But to say scientific is not to speak of the paraphernalia and techniques of the laboratory; it is to say realistic and rational—empirically grounded and self-corrective in application. Policy is scientific when it is formed by the free use of intelligence on the materials of experience.[8]

The touchstone to a revised policy sciences, then, is not a lockstep adherence to positivist methodologies, for instance, employing welfare economics to study homelessness, simply because they have certain theoretical aspirations or deal in empirical criteria or variables. Those methodologies have already indicated their limitations in theory, data, and results. Likewise, few studies of technology policy can limit themselves to strictly technical issues, as Bruce L. R. Smith's study of the presidential scientific advisory systems has demonstrated.[9] More pertinently, Helen Ingram and Steven R. Smith have recently presented a series of public policy designs constructed explicitly to encourage people to act in democratic manners, arguing that "policy analysts are now moving . . . to consider policies, strategies, and actions to make democracy work better, . . . [and] examine the impact of policy on citizenship and democracy,"[10] a policy sciences *for* democracy, if one pleases. The proposition therefore calls for a much broader range of approaches, more than a true multidisciplinary exercise based upon a menu of conceptual visions but a true multiepistemological activity, because, as we shall see, there could easily be multiple "solutions" to the problem, as a function of the investigatory lenses, many of which might be otherwise overlooked. Most important, the methodologies should be defined by the problem, with a principal focus on recommendations that serve to enhance democratic processes.

Carol Hirschon Weiss makes a similar argument, one based on "objectivity" and intent rather than on the more acceptable catchphrases such as "scientific" and "empirical":

A critical distinction . . . is the difference between more and less objectivity. There is a distinction between research that strives for fair and comprehensive analysis of an issue and research that sets out—either consciously or through lack of self-critical reflection—to "make a case" for a position. A hallmark of science is the attempt to disprove, or in Popper's term falsify, one's assumptions. . . . If research leads to findings that convince the researcher of the superiority of one particular course, that's fine. But to start out to prove a case is the function of the ideologue, lobbyist, or hired gun, not the policy researcher.[11]

An example would be illuminating. Compare, for instance, two renderings of a condition almost as venerable as politics themselves, political corruption. Robert Klitgaard's otherwise excellent *Controlling Corruption* study views corruption largely as an economic phenomenon (in other words, personal monetary gains derived from falsifying customs declarations or systematically abusing income tax statements), one designed to enrich the pockets of those involved.[12] He naturally puts great stock then in the Philippine expression for corruption, *lagay*, or "speed money," that is, illegally exchanging currency for ill-gotten goods or services.[a] Klitgaard accordingly poses his recommendations in terms of the economic theory of moral hazard and principal agents, or how a supervisor can monitor an "agent's" work so as to preclude corruption.[13] However, principal agents theory cannot explain corruption in which the actors realize little if any monetary—as opposed to political—gain (as was the case in the Watergate fiasco and, twenty-five years later, the Iran-*contra* affair), nor how to sustain durable barriers to corrupt behavior, because corruption and its cures transcend strictly economic analysis and remedy. In historical point of fact, we find that additional recommendations posed by principal agents theory—such as enhanced layers of supervision—have not prevented subsequent incidents of corruption, regardless of the administration. The multiple cases of federal-

---

[a] When it was revealed that Charles R. Keating, one of the most egregious perpetrators of the Savings & Loan crisis of the 1980s, had donated large amount of to the campaigns of five U.S. senators (the so-called Keating Five), he was asked to explain. His response is characterized by its chutzpah: "One question . . . many raised in recent weeks had to do with whether my financial support in any way influenced several political figures to take up my cause. I want to say in the most forceful way I can: I certainly hope so." Keating's contributions clearly qualify as *lagay*. Quoted in P. deLeon (1993, p. 153).

level political corruption during the 1980s were carried out in spite of the Watergate-inspired oversight legislation, such as the Ethics in Government Act, the special prosecutor, and a press already alerted to the journalistic prizes attached to the discovery of corruption in elevated places.

In contrast, Peter deLeon's *Thinking About Political Corruption* treats political corruption in a policy sciences mode, that is, as a multifaceted condition with its roots sunk equally in economics (i.e., pecuniary benefits), political science (ability to rule), psychology, sociology (functional aspects), and the law.[14] The sociologist Robert K. Merton thoughtfully argues that incidents of political corruption could be viewed as serving both a structural and a functional basis when government services are lacking or seen as inadequate: "the functional deficiencies of the official structure generate an alternative (unofficial) structure to fulfill existing needs somewhat more efficiently."[15] The political scientists James Scott and Michael Johnston similarly view corruption as a means to circumvent bureaucratic obstacles or what they call organizational "bottlenecks."[16] These perspectives, combined with the more standard economic motives, suggest a much richer set of explanations for political corruption. Furthermore, the multiple perspectives indicate why it has proven impossible to eradicate, for corruption can often be seen as the product of seemingly well-meaning officials or citizens searching with their own vision of justification for elusive public efficiencies; in other words, it represents a priority of expedition over equity in an attempt to circumvent time-consuming, inefficient, and very public (read: disabling) government procedures. Rear Adm. John Poindexter, in explaining his willingness to patently deceive Congress as it investigated his role in the Iran-*contra* episode, explained how he came to set aside his sworn obligation as an officer in the U.S. Navy to uphold the Constitution in order to implement a highly dubious foreign policy action (i.e., trading munitions to a "terrorist" state in exchange for hostages, with the proceeds going to rebel Sandinista forces embargoed by Congress); as he testified before Congress:

> I simply did not want any outside interference. The problem, as I have stated, I didn't want Congress to know the details of how we were implementing the President's policy.[17]

As such, the standard economists' corruption cures (relying on principal agents theory) call for more oversight or regulation, and could turn out to be counterproductive. These, in turn, might well serve to create more bottlenecks, thereby exacerbating the problem and leading to increased incidents of political corruption, only at a higher cost! And, at day's end, one is left with the warning of the Tower Commission that investigated the Iran-*contra* affairs, one more political or social than economic in nature: quoting the Roman poet, Juvenal, the final report asked, "Who shall guard the guardians from themselves?" All of these central considerations fall outside the disciplinary ken of the economist studying political corruption.

The multidisciplinary approach also argues for a more variegated and effective menu of policy options for combating political corruption than any single approach can muster. Political scientists address organizations and processes while Merton cautions in a functionalist vein: "any attempt to eliminate an existing social structure without providing adequate alternative structures for fulfilling the functions previously fulfilled by the abolished organization is doomed to failure." [18] Economic disincentives are unquestionably critical but still incomplete in a political world; as Susan Rose-Ackerman, herself an economist, cautions,

> An effort to use economists' methods to synthesize political scientists' concerns ultimately forces us to recognize the limitations of the economists' approach itself. While information and competition may often reduce corrupt incentives, they cannot completely substitute for the personal integrity of political actors. [19]

It is, then, the combination of disciplinary perspectives and insights that presents a more realistic opportunity to understand social and political complexities and, concomitantly, to derive policy recommendations. By the same token, the policy sciences require numerous research approaches keeping in mind their respective roles as pieces of a multifaceted policy puzzle. In point of workaday practice, this is usually how exemplary policy research is engaged, with (say) statisticians, economists, political scientists, and sociologists all working cooperatively, synergetically on a single complex policy issue. The RAND Corporation's study at the beginning of President Clinton's administration on the role of homosexuals in the American armed forces is a splendid but largely singular illustration of just such an exercise. [20]

The problem is that, at present, there is no generally accepted, overarching policy sciences paradigm that steadfastly encourages such a multidisciplinary mode tailored to the specific policy issues at hand, except for the conventional wisdom that public policy problems in their natural setting almost never subscribe to a single disciplinary position. For instance, the current discussions over institutional "downsizing" or "out-sourcing" (in both the public and private sectors) is usually reported as an economic issue but the causes, displacements, and ramifications go well beyond the economists' texts and intimately affect such issues as employee morale, personal stability, and public trust. Most academic and training programs, for all their interdisciplinary posturing, clearly emphasize one discipline or approach over the others. Operationally, the impetus is less focused in theory or education and more in piecemeal practice which, however successful or dismal, leaves little didactic residue for future learning.

These issues, however, have long been standard complaints, that policy research is too disciplined in its approach and too limited in its scope. Further exhortations along those lines will likely be as sterile and unproductive as past complaints. On the contrary, what is needed is an alternative formulation of the policy sciences, that is, a model directed toward Lasswellian democratic goals while espousing an altered operating philosophy than the restricted philosophy of positivism. To those ends, let us now turn to examinations of some newer policy research orientations that largely operate within the somewhat loosened (as opposed to the more traditional) boundaries of positivism. Following these, we will turn to an analysis of postpositivism and critical theory. The purpose is to identify (at least partially) the means by which postpositivism can offer particular support to a participatory policy sciences, which we shall demonstrate to be a more democratic policy sciences.

New Policy Research Paradigms

In recent years, a number of policy scientists within the American policy research community have been slowly evolving from the economic man model, since at least the early 1970s. Policy scientists attempted to jury-rig the positivist paradigm to take into account the unknown and unmanageable policy elements. Some policy analysts were trying to retain its "rational" characteristics while accommodating its less quantitative components, such as reflecting certain "interpretative" shadings to empirical policy research. Others, such as David C. Paris and James F. Reynolds, drawing on the sociology of knowledge literature, argued that one could examine the relative worth among policies by measuring their comparative, internal degrees of rationality.[21] Still other scholars, such as Gian-domenico Majone and Frank Fischer, have brought more of a rhetor-ical flavor to analysis, indicating that the posed argument could be just as pivotal as the actual analysis.[22] And, finally, other policy re-search has returned to Lasswell's policy model as a means to im-prove our understanding of the component phrases of the policy process (e.g., policy formulation or agenda setting), many times us-ing case study materials.[23]

More recently, models of policy change have been proposed that still rely on the positivist school but make specific concessions for el-ements not generally viewed as within the positivism domain, such as "core" and "policy core" values. These values are social and group constructs that the authors allow are indeed influential in policy deliberations; they are, however, relatively slow to change or even amend, with policy gestation periods running up to ten to fifteen years. To most politicians, policy analysts, and policymakers, these are unacceptable time frames, if for no other reason, the majority of the participants will have assumed new roles and thus lost whatever policy momentum might have accumulated.

Paul A. Sabatier and Hank C. Jenkins-Smith advance an "advo-cacy coalition framework" model that purports to indicate policy changes over the course of at least a decade as policy participants are slowly persuaded by increasing evidence (often scientific in content) to alter their core and policy beliefs; their most salient examples are from the environmental arena. Frank R. Baumgartner and Bryan D. Jones describe a set of policy conditions (which they call "equilibria") that remain relatively stable until sufficient opposing arguments are marshaled such that the old policy environment is forced into a state of disequilibrium, or (drawing upon archaeology) what they call a system characterized by "punctuated equilibria"; after the pol-icy dust has settled, conditions return to an altered but again stable condition.[24]

Although these authors are proposing serious amendments to the traditional positivist paradigm—for instance, both are openly attempting to predict how policies change, usually as a function of a change in public values—at base they are continuing to subscribe to its rational logic, procedures, and assumptions. Their fundamental implication is that if only people think a little harder, develop a bit more data, or were a tad more "rational," they would arrive at a con-sensual change in policy positions and subsequent implementations. These models are perfectly appropriate for policy situations where the ends are certain and the means are both variable and limited (e.g., paving an interstate highway from point A to point B). But they are depressingly inadequate when both ends and means are uncertain or undetermined (e.g., paving the same highway from here to there, with both "locations" subject to political determinations). In the latter instance, the traditional policy sciences can offer information that *might* improve the decision making but whether it *will* improve the decision making is anybody's guess.

The ecology of the policy sciences, which is almost surely to blame for this state of indecision, has been characterized by Yehezkel Dror as being populated with concerns over "fuzzy gambling," in other words, an environment in which it is impossible to calculate the probabilities of specific actions, and, moreover, one did not even know the consequences of those actions because of a series of internal and inherent conflicts between the two major driving forces—intellectual knowledge and political reality, both of which are subject to their own peculiar dynamics.[25]

In Sabatier and Jenkins-Smith's advocacy coalition formulation, the authors' presumption of player rationality (i.e., identifiable self-interest) juxtaposed with the exclusion of subjectivity, with values being presented in an a priori distinction between "core" and "policy core" values, represents a dicey prognosis for prediction. When, for example, in their model, does a crossover point between these two value regimes take place and what is its effect upon policy, or how does one determine the difference between the two before the case? All told, these frameworks do not take us very far from their roots in positivism.

There are a growing number of policy authors who continue to argue that although the positivist model is basically incomplete and that it requires additional information and perceptions from other viewpoints, a positivist policy paradigm remains possible, even though it would be much less dependent on the rational actor model than those previously described. If for no other reason, these not-quite-postpositivists are in general agreement that one of the most crucial demands for greater information comes from the policy recipients themselves, rather than just the policy analysts, as demands growing out of the American civil rights and the local education movements have exemplified. The revised question then becomes three: what methodologies are more salient, for what reasons, and to whom?

Martin Rein has posed various versions of what he calls a frame-reflective model. It is based on the postpositivist refusal to honor the positivist value-fact separation, or what he called a "value-critical[b] approach [that] subjects goals and values to critical review." Drawing upon the European sociology of knowledge heritage, Rein emphasizes the predominant presence but tacit invisibility of the normative elements in policy-making. He makes the central argument that a value-critical analysis must draw upon a resolution based on an idiographic as opposed to nomothetic (i.e., the treatment of events toward formulating generalizable theories) perspective:

> The value-critical approach takes the line that values are not simply wishes and desires but are grounded in a fundamental structure which is central to real processes; and they can therefore become a meaningful subject of debate.[26]

In other words, Rein is explicitly adopting the postpositivist perspective in which ends (values) are to be just as exposed to analysis as means—indeed, they are too important to be left in a state of implicit assumption or, even worse, an unexamined normative lacuna. Rein's preferred set of policy illustrations are deftly extracted from comparative social welfare programs, whose normative conflicts obviously fit handily into his model.

Therefore, Rein (often with his MIT colleague Donald Schön) proposes the importance of a policy "story-telling" or a narrative analysis (what they are later to call "mapping and framing," or what distinguishes "fact" from opinion) to set the preconditions that favor (or oppose, for that matter) a set of policy recommendations.[27] Deborah A. Stone subsequently advocated a similar narrative methodology in response to her critique of "efficiency," "effectiveness," and other positivist criteria, which she terms the "rationality project."[28] Again, these exercises emphasizing the policy environment lend substance to Lasswell's earlier contextual suggestions.

Rein is undoubtedly correct when he assumes that analysis can never be treated as independent of the values the analyst or client holds. But, having said that, Rein finally is confronted with what he terms "the problem of objectivity," that is, "how we can prevent our ideology from distorting our understanding of the reality that we seek to explain and alter. . . . No one can claim privileged exemption from distortion; the problem is how to guard against it."[29] He and Schön later admit: "We know of no well-described examples of frame-

---

[b]Which Rein sets in opposition to a "value-committed" approach (i.e., the more rationalist posture) or the "value-neutral" approach (i.e., pure science).

reflective policy discourse."[30] This "shortcoming," of course, is exactly what is missing in much of postpositivism, a field in which ideology, values, and belief become part and parcel of the formal analysis. Furthermore, like other postpositivist analysis, frame-reflective or value-critical analysis brings sufficient ambiguity into the analytic operation that the ability of the concept to reach policy closure is in doubt and that its results becomes clouded. For starters: how is the analysis bounded or how can "story telling" be calibrated and compared? But the important idea of Rein and his colleagues remain constant: individual values are just as open to analysis as are the relative "facts," and must similarly be open to public discourse.

Maarten A. Hajer brings the concept of a "discourse coalition" to the policy sciences' table, specifically dealing with environmental policy and how European governments have coped with acid rain. In his usage, a discourse coalition

> is basically a group of actors who share a social construct. . . . Discourse here is defined as an ensemble of ideas, concepts, and categories through which meaning is given to phenomena. Discourses frame certain problems; that is to say, they distinguish some aspects of a situation rather than others. . . . A discourse coalition approach suggests that politics is a process in which different actors from various backgrounds from specific coalitions around specific story lines.[31]

In explaining how different discourses ("ensembles") come to prominence, Hajer is attempting to put Rein and Stone's stories or narratives into a more formalized construct. However, Hajer's current framework needs greater elaboration, for it is not immediately clear how his analysis is significantly different than an excellent case study except for the use of a newer, postpositivism vocabulary. Indeed, the concept of a discourse coalition offers further credibility to authors with a positivist bent, like Sabatier and Jenkins-Smith with their advocacy coalitions, for all are dealing with policy changes, differing only in how their relative means are examined and coalitions formed. Hajer's particular contribution is a more explicit orchestrating of a wider choir of policy voices, that is, those outside the immediate circle of interest groups, into a policy chorus.

In short, the thrust of the alternative policy approaches that fall somewhat short of postpositivism has a number of commonalities. The various methodologies all deemphasize the policy sciences' traditional reliance upon the empirical, positivist modes (to a greater or lesser extent) as they emphasize that other, non-(but not ir-) rational information is at least (but not always more) relevant. At the same time, they stress the need for multiple perspectives and for attention to differing times, places, perspectives, and individuals. Lastly, they bring several items to the policy medium (e.g., the necessity of multiple perspectives) that explicitly encourage the policy sciences' model to a greater agreement with democratic means and ends, even though this is not always part of the explicit understanding.

Postpositivism

It is difficult to pin down precisely where or when postpositivism was originated, just as it is difficult to tie down a starting date for the positivism it was intended to supplant. Most observers of the philosophy of science put the positivism's genesis somewhere during the Age of the Enlightenment in Western Europe (roughly from the seventeenth century to the early nineteenth century), and probably peaking in its social science applications under the influence of logical positivism (around the turn of the twentieth century). Basically, positivism attempts to apply the lessons and procedures of the physical sciences to the social sciences' settings, trying to extract and codify universal laws and their responding behaviors. The essence of positivism has been well stated by Douglas Torgerson:

> The positive spirit would rigorously distance itself from the speculations of theology and metaphysics, confronting the world objectively in order to observe the facts and determine the lawful order of nature and society. The domain of mystery and ambiguity would be abandoned in order to know what could be known clearly and certainly. . . . Knowledge would replace politics. [32]

Thus, one finds positivism associated with many of the luminary European sociologists, such as Auguste Comte, Henri Saint-Simon, and certainly Karl Marx, as well as with most of the great English and French political and economic theorists, including John Locke, Adam Smith, John Stuart Mill, and Montesquieu. [33]

Positivism has had incalculable effects concerning both philosophy and methodology in American political science (most notably with the behavioral revolution of the 1960s), modern (i.e., postpolitical) economics, and, of most concern to us here, the policy sciences. The pursuit of positivism implied that the individual might well have been the primary unit of analysis but only as a convenient metric; individuals were measured as voting statistics, rational persons and utility aggregators, or as demographic entities. As such, they were treated as little more than descriptive numbers in a series of "objective" policy equations, something to be manipulated toward political goals or societal utility maximizations that were almost surely not theirs as individuals.

The effects of positivism in the policy sciences can clearly be seen in the development of public management theories in the United States. Beginning with Frederick Taylor's time and motion studies and running through various scientific management iterations like management by objectives (MBO) and PPBS, the management literature gives easy rise to such a mechanical interpretation with a distinct sentiment opposed to democratic procedures. For instance, a detached, scientific observation practice Deborah A. Stone refers to as "clinical reason" "elevates a particular type of expert knowledge and denigrates or even ignores the knowledge, perceptions, and interpretations of ordinary citizens in their relations with other individuals and with social institutions." Thus, clinical reason acts to transform "social problems into clinical syndromes [that are] profoundly undemocratic."[34] Theorists in rational choice (political science), institutional rational choice (public administration), and public choice (economics) have assumed much the same posture.

But perhaps more important that the positivist's general philosophy applied to governance were the ways by which it was operationalized, the assumptions it logically posited, and the appearance of "truth" it presented. Perhaps the classic statement of the positivist influence on public affairs was the seeming distinction between fact and value. Public administrators were sorely enjoined over the greater part of this century—originally by none other than Woodrow Wilson, the first great author in American public administration—to deal exclusively in the realm of demonstrable "fact" in administrative affairs while leaving the politicians to deal with more subjective (or less "scientific") "values." Therefore, during most of its tenure, public administration has been intellectually unable to address the larger social and political issues or goals that social technology was being asked to pursue, at least in part because of its general acceptance of the positivist orientation. Even stronger ascriptions to positivism may be made for political science, psychology, economics, and, by extension, the policy sciences.

Few of the positivist precepts were ultimately to hold true for the social sciences but their intuitive appeal and, hence, their predominant effects on the study of public affairs were unmistakable. One hardly ever hears of government programs or public administration theory that are neither established nor evaluated in terms outside of cost-efficiencies, a concept central to positivism and now considered by many to be a problematic criterion. Carol Hirschon Weiss suggests that the social research community deliberately has donned the physical sciences' raiments of scientific knowledge, that is, a surrogate for scientific truth, as a way to protect itself from the charge of uninhibited advocacy or lackadaisical analysis.[35] Most analysts, it seems, preferred using costs as the analytic currency, the "bottom line" as it were, because most people could agree on costs, or so it was thought.

The social sciences, however, were to prove to be a far testier laboratory than the physical sciences' tools could bring to bear. Indeed, it was the physical scientists themselves who first indicated that their methodologies were sometimes inadequate to study their chosen phenomena; Werner Heisenburg's Uncertainty Principle, the debate over quantum mechanics highlighted by Neils Bohr and Copenhagen Interpretation, and Kurt Gödel's Incompleteness theorem in mathematics all indicated that the precisions the physical scientists sought had much to learn about their own world. It was therefore somewhat presumptuous to import their philosophy and methodologies into another world, one increasingly seen as very different, as Dror's "fuzzy gambling" metaphor reminds us.

Torgerson describes this nagging inability to reduce the policy world to probabilistic projections because of the tension between the two major components:

> The dynamic nature of the [policy sciences] phenomenon is rooted in an internal tension, a *dialectical opposition between knowledge and politics*. Through the interplay of knowledge and politics, different aspects of the phenomenon become salient at different moments. . . . The presence of dialectical tension means that the phenomenon has the potential to develop, to change its form.[36]

In effect, the conditions confronting the social sciences were correctly suggesting their own analogies—if not answers—to Heisenberg's Uncertainty Theorem. More troubling, of course, is the search for a resolution.

This disquietude was reinforced with the variety of postpositivist inroads being made by such concepts as deconstructionist theories (as advanced by, among others, Michel Foucault), hermeneutics (with Martin Heidegger and Hans-Georg Gadamer), and other, similarly interpretivist schools.[37] Although these share many similarities, we shall examine them individually to understand how they differ from positivist methodologies as well as what they offer in terms of alternative policy constructs.

In the deconstructionist perspective, "fact" is constantly open for interpretation and reinterpretation as a function of time, conditions, professional position, and other variables beyond the "scientific" bounds of positivism (which, of course, are not recognized as "scientific"). Torgerson sets out the altered emphases: "Whatever portrays itself as ultimate becomes portrayed as arbitrary, and its privilege is thereby thrown into question . . . instability arises as the constructions are shown to be partial, insufficient in themselves."[38] In his essay on "governmentality," Michel Foucault emphasizes how changing social and political conditions from the time of the Italian Renaissance had affected the ways in which European statecraft viewed Machiavelli's treatise on *The Prince*.[39]

Deconstructionists perceive parameters, variables, procedures, even "facts" as social and political (as opposed to Divine) artifacts. Marie Danziger observes that since "the standards of judgment, canons of evidence, or normative measures are proscribed by his or her professional community . . . the potential for professional scientific objectivity, political neutrality, or substantive change are, by definition, curtailed significantly." These alternatives are multiplied by the understanding that the forum for discussion is now greatly enlarged with no set rule for exclusion. And, finally, language itself is taken to task, for "Ultimately [deconstructionism] is calling attention to the language of policy analysis, which, if taken for granted, conceals the potential to limit, exclude, distort, and manipulate."[40] But this diversity brings with it a definite downside, namely, as Torgerson concludes, "By stressing the arbitrary features of any stable point of reference, deconstruction would introduce a question mark into any coherent approach to policy, including any seeking to follow the path of deconstruction."[41] There are, quite deliberately, no consistent bench marks or dividing lines outlining a deconstructionist protocol (or, especially for a constructionist regime) and, thus, no "truths" (impeachable or otherwise) or "facts," realizations standing in complete contradiction to tenets of positivism. One could also inquire as to the inherent frustrations of discussing a deconstructionist agenda in which the endgame is always beyond the next perspective.

John S. Dryzek defines hermeneutics policy analysis "as the

evaluations of existing conditions and the exploration of alternatives to them, in term of criteria derived from an understanding of possible better conditions, through an interchange between the frames of reference of analysis and actors."[42] In many ways, hermeneutics is an exegetic exercise, which assumes, after Gadamer, that one's view of the world is fundamentally linguistic, an approach in which goals, views, and histories are not necessarily commonly held but the centrality of the perspectives themselves are always shared among those concerned citizens. In Roberto Alejandro's description:

> In light of Gadamer's hermeneutics . . . when we analyze a text or past event, we cannot proceed as the scientist claims to do. We cannot erase our own historical perspective, which means that we cannot abandon the principles and doctrines that define our identify and nurture our moral character.

As a mean of conceptualization, hermeneutics places a priority on the individual's perspective as opposed to the state's. The distinction between hermeneutics and the "scientific method" becomes unmistakable when considering the ambiguities inherent in interpretation:

> Interpretation is always a construction of meaning, which is what distinguishes the scientist's endeavor from hermeneutics' purpose. The scientist seeks certainly; hermeneutics seeks "clarity." . . . The construction of meaning has to consider the boundaries provided by the text itself as well as the background provided by the traditions that made it possible.[43]

As was the case with the deconstructionist view, hermeneutics stands in contrast to the scientific basis of learning, results, and discovered "truths," in its emphasis on individual visions and interpretations, as well as having a higher tolerance level for uncertainty. However, it finally runs into problems concerned with the shoals of validation; how does somebody "know" something under constantly changing hermeneutics regime,[c] which gets one into a "hermenetic circle," from which there is no easy exit. Still, its diverse foci and its emphasis on contextual analysis draws hermeneutic analysis closer to the Lasswellian policy sciences paradigm.

---

[c] A hermenuetist would naturally object to being held hostage to idea of validity, which is basically a positivist criterion.

The interpretive school tends to involve a wider range of policy-relevant phenomena than the rationalist school or even hermeneutics. Dvora Yanow defines this interpretive perspective as

> a focus on the discrepancies or divergences between stated policies and the lived experience of the policies . . . typically those entailed in an instrumentally rational model of human acts. . . . [An interpretative perspective] entails the difficult task of seeing what is *not there or hearing what is not said*. . . .

Moreover, these processes frequently involve the policy audience becoming "active constructors of meaning, and thus active participants in a process in which they may choose to play a role as well as they may choose to be nonparticipant."[44] Hence, the interpretive approach not only involves a broader set of analytic conditions and indicators but also an important element in terms of a greater democratic process. Interpretive analysis brings with it a strong emphasis on expanding the participants and symbols of policy research and programs to include those parties whose circumstances are most directly affected, what we earlier called the "targeted audience," rather than only those who purchase political access. But it does present the inevitable question of where the analytic domain or actors become relatively irrelevant (which an interpretivist would surely claim as violating the very idea), again with generally scant means for resolution.

As we have just seen, these postpositivist schools share many commonalities but they have not yet managed to displace completely the rationalist foundation of the policy sciences. Perhaps the rationalist traditions are too entrenched to jettison but, more than likely, the indeterminacy of these newer approaches' processes and results is the more likely obstacle. Let us examine more closely hermeneutics as a representative example of a postpositivist brand of policy analysis. At some point, the traditional analyst can declare with some confidence that (say) a benefit-cost analysis is completed; granted, it probably has not included all relevant partners or explored all aspects (e.g., the question of who holds legal standing), but at some point in time (admittedly an arguable point for quite legitimate reasons), it is pretty much "done" or completed according to most observers.

To be sure, it might not be an optimal solution within a given frame of reference but the resources necessary to advance it toward that goal would almost certainly not be commensurate with the added increments of effort, a situation economists refer to a "second best" condition (one in which it is not renumerative to devote additional resources toward optimality). It would be, to use Herbert Simon's classic expression, a "satisficing" (i.e., satisfying and sufficient) resolution.

This analytic end point is much harder to determine when a wider, hermeneutic spectrum of opinions and perspectives are sought, a larger number of "clients" are included, and a more differentiated set of methodologies is proposed. Under hermeneutics, whose goods, whose values, and whose contexts are always pertinent and always subject to change, as opposed to positivism, which works to make parameters relatively constant. In hermeneutics, the analyst cannot be disassociated from the analysis, as "objectivity" becomes a hollow word. One may ultimately achieve "clarity" but many would ask at what cost and in what time frame.

The pivotal epistemological question—when is enough information enough?—is impossible to determine on a relatively absolute or predetermined basis for either the positivist or the postpositivist, but particularly for the latter. For an area of inquiry that prides itself on the timeliness of its options and recommendations to authority—of speaking truth to power in a restricted time frame—this ambiguity could be fatal. Facing a choice between "precisely wrong" or "ambiguously noncommittal," one suspects that government offices and analysts would prefer the precision now, worry about its "wrongness" later, and forget about the noncommittal.

Finally, we need to remind ourselves that, at least in the social sciences, there are no objectively determined "best" approaches even when we are comparing the positivist and postpositivist arenas; as Torgerson notes, "It should further be recognized that the adoption of *any* methodological posture—whether right or wrong—is inescapably a form of political action. The gulf between the expert and the citizen thus appears not as politically neutral, but as an artifact of the administrative state,"[45] which invariably is held hostage by the existing (or possibly the ascendant) political interest groups. All of these shortcomings are addressed by the postpositivist movements, which identify these deficiencies if not necessarily providing the remedies.

Still, the question obviously arises for the policy analyst: in an environment in which rationality is a dubious proposition, values are amorphous and rarely explicated, and politics consciously left to the political decision-maker, how reliant should policy researchers be on positivist procedures that fundamentally absorb all of these unknowns as knowns, or at best, subsumes them in a set of (usually) unspoken but not unimportant assumptions? More to the central point, why should policymakers accept serious recommendations from their policy staffs that consciously exclude these usually pivotal considerations? And, lastly, should they continue to work in a policy sciences that increasingly resembles a retreat from its earliest democratic principles?

Critical Theory

Critical theory may be characterized as a methodology and a philosophy, with both approaches most often associated with the German Frankfurt School.[46] In the United States, the contributions of critical theory to postpositivism in terms of the policy sciences have most often been associated with the work of Jürgen Habermas and his interpreters.[47]

Habermas argues in general that inquiries carried out within the social sciences are too often restricted in their scope of examination or investigation. They typically view the world through an artificially limited, constrained set of (usually) disciplinary perspectives. In particular, he suggests that a highly rational, technocratic-oriented perspective omits much in the nature of a person's value structure, omissions that can frequently and seriously skew the results. Again, the supposition is not that a rationalistic discipline (or, in fact, any single discipline) is inherent wrong; rather, that any singular analysis is inherently incomplete.

More critically, as Daniel Yankelovich has written, Habermas proposes that "knowledge conceived as a body of facts and truths existing apart from human purpose is a myth."[48] He contends, in implicit agreement with Harold Lasswell's statement of the policy sciences, that there are multiple perspectives and purposes to a problem (what Habermas often calls a "crisis") that need to be simultaneously coexamined. Finally, according to Jane Braaten, the "critical theories of society . . . identify deep conflicts, or potentials for society-wide crises, inherent within the social, political, and economic institutions of modern capitalist societies."[49] That is, the conflicts can be concurrently therapeutic and diagnostic in their normative context, presenting a set of opposing dynamics that must be reflected in an analysis of the crisis.

Habermas bases his social philosophy on the context or environment surrounding a particular crisis, with special emphasis on what he calls "communicative rationality," which he sets in opposition to "instrumental rationality." John Forester has observed that the concept of instrumental rationality—what Habermas terms "empirical-analytic science," the first of his three forms of knowledge—is perfectly "appropriate to conventionally technical problems; however, it cannot address questions of value formation, value change, social growth, or learning,"[50] that is, the valuative heart of the policy sciences.

Communicative rationality, on the other hand, "is to be used to explain how social interaction in general is possible and, a fortiori, the evolution of specific social arrangements and institutions," an arrangement Habermas clearly directs toward a democratic orientation. His declaration of an "intersubjective understanding" (*Verstehen*), or what we might describe as feelings and motives, is his second form of knowledge. It basically underpins cooperation within a communicative rational action framework and represents, according to Braaten,

> communication between participants attempting to reach a rational consensus. . . . Communication is inherently oriented towards mutual understanding, and the standards that govern communications are therefore conditioned upon reaching mutual understanding and, ideally, rational consequences.[51]

In the lexicon of the policy sciences, Habermas has presented over a number of years a strategy that moves toward such issues as how people arrive at social change and policy learning through social discourse as opposed to political power. In this sense, he stands in the theoretical avant-garde to many involved in contemporary research in the policy sciences of democracy. In these terms, Habermas is projecting his final and, if one believes Yankelovich, possibly most important category of knowledge, an "emancipatory" side designed "to make people free, to emancipate them mentally from false forms of consciousness, ideology, prejudice, and mental coercion."[52]

In one of Habermas's more celebrated phrases, the political and social worlds suffer from "systematically distorted communications," in which (to oversimplify), one party (or coalition) has a clear and persistent dominance in a policy arena over other relevant parties and avails itself of that authority (e.g., interest groups or governmental agencies). In Habermas's concept, this distribution leads to a "one-sided rationalization," one that does not occur as a random act of nature but as an overt political mechanism, one undermining communicative rationality. While this scenario is often a government-imposed condition, it can develop, Braaten cautions, from a self-inflicted state that Habermas terms the "colonization of the life-world";[d] in other words,

> the tendency of systems in modern welfare states to take over [personal] lifeworld functions is a result of public demand—demand for administrative repairs to the disruptions to the lifeworld caused by fluctuations and other developments in the economy.[53]

Historically, this represents the age-old conflict between the government (with its bureaucratic arm) and its citizens, and the obvious bias that relationship engenders. Habermas would suggest that a state of systemically distorted communication leads to some level of inequity within the polity, with little doubt that the inequity would not be ascribed to distorting agency. Bobrow and Dryzek cogently capture the essence of critical thinking's conceptualization when they suggest that it "devotes itself to the elimination of distortion, which can occur through suppression, debasement, or deception. . . . [It is] grounded in the investigator's conception of the felt needs and deprivations of a group of individuals."[54]

In its stead, Habermas and his proponents propose a more discursive, dialogic pattern between parties, one predicated on his concept of "communicative competence." In this mode, Habermas features the postulation of an "ideal speech situation" that (especially in its idealized form[e]) emphasizes a relatively open policy discourse and forum in which four preconditions prevail among the participants as validity claims that define the ideal speech situation:

- *communicative* speech acts imply what a speaker says is understandable to all the relevant actors;
- *representative* speech acts imply truth and sincerity, that is, people say what they mean without the threat of coercion and they are to be trusted;
- *regulative* speech acts imply that their normative content is legitimate, and that values are just as relevant as "facts"; and
- *constative* speech acts imply the ability to provide interpretative and explanatory analysis such that, in the long run, every party is heard free of communicative distortion.

---

[d] "Lifeworld" was borrowed by Habermas from the phenomenological writings of Edmund Husserl to indicate a shared social reality.

[e] Habermas's "ideal speech situation" is an issue of some controversy over exactly what he means (or does not mean) to suggest. Rather than being taken literally (and perhaps misleadingly), it is proposed here that an ideal speech situation is a never-to-be achieved measure indicating a normative goal.

Habermas, according to Roy Kemp, "maintains that these formal properties, derived from his formal analysis of the rational foundations of everyday speech, alone guarantee that a rationally grounded consensus can emerge from practical discourse."[55] For a number of institutional and personal reasons, an idea speech condition is chimerical, but even then it serves as a means to calibrate the extent of, or fidelity to, communicative rationality. (It is important to observe that "rationality" to Habermas is a function of free inquiry, reflection, and discourse, rather than the positivist use of the word.) These then are the criteria for communicative competence.

The end result of Habermas's communicative competence is, inevitably, a more participatory democratic system. Based upon Habermas, John Dryzek enunciates a principle of "discursive democracy," in which "discursive" indicates that "No concerned individuals should be excluded, and, if necessary, some educative mechanisms should promote the competent participation of persons with a material interest in the issues at hand who might otherwise be left out."[56] In Daniel Yankelovich's words,

> Habermas is quite insistent . . . that a genuine communication in a democracy can take place only when all forms of domination—overt and hidden—have been removed. . . . The goals of communicative action are to permit us to comprehend each other well enough so that common goals and understandings are possible. In Habermas' view, communicative action is the key to building a democratic consensus.[57]

Mark Warren echoes these goals, when he emphasizes that "The point of democracy, in Habermas' view, is not simply to reconcile conflicting interests . . . but to design institutions that encourage discourse, which, in turn, is necessary to identify and distinguish plural, common, and emergent interests."[58]

While few of a democratic disposition would argue against such "obvious" reasoning, the applications of Habermas's proscribed communicative competence and its democratic orientation are far from everyday or straightforward. Even when special allowances are made to include other parties, the outcomes are usually determined by the bureaucracy that has special access to particular information. More important, the bureaucracy can structure the forum and procedures pointing toward its predetermined conclusions, which effectively deny the democratic posture. The reasoning is not hard to fathom; the various "at risk" administrative agencies would have the most to lose from an established protocol of communicative rationality because their authority would seemingly be compromised and their existence endangered.

These conditions characterized two energy-oriented public fora—the English public hearings on the Windscale nuclear reprocessing plant and the Carter administration's domestic policy review of solar energy[59]—that emphasized the testimony of persons from outside the official energy bureaucracy. However open and discursive their nominal purposes, the respective decisions were still heavily slanted in favor of the government. Kemp (his own particular bias shining brightly through) summarizes his findings of the Windscale inquiries (which closely mirror those of Laird):

> [P]ublic inquiries rather serve to legitimize the actions and interests of dominant groups in advanced capitalist societies. Outcomes of public hearings are rarely objective, rational, and egalitarian; they are manipulated to further the interests of both state and capital. . . . I contend that a primary mechanism through which this is achieved is the *systematic distortion of the communications process* that takes place at public inquiries . . . [Moreover], this is merely another move in the attempt to depoliticize the public sphere by appealing to the *democratic nature of public hearings* in order to gain justificatory force when the legitimacy of such an appeal may well be suspect.[60]

The arguments decrying critical theory are patent—critical theory is thought to be unrealistic, since there are numerous reasons why bureaucracies and interest groups could (and probably would) work to maintain the status quo, that is, to undermine what level of communicative competence that was created, even assuming that policymakers might engage in an exercise in critical theory, as Kemp's example highlights. Established administrative domains (with concomitant ties to influential groups outside the bureaucracy) would be endangered by new and largely untried analytic methodologies whose very purposes were uncertain. Others, such as Sanford F. Schram, criticize Habermas's thesis of communicative rationality as being too removed from the practical politics of the policy process; in short, Schram claims that critical theory is unconcerned or too dismissive of the pivotal political machinations.[61] As with the other postpositivist approaches, one needs to inquire as to just who chooses which parties should be included, which could be a major debate itself. In sum, there would seem to be a welter of opposing theoretic and practical arguments against the idea of communicative competence.

The standard counterexample of an extended deliberative forum—the efforts of Mr. Justice Thomas Berger (who chaired what
came to be known as the Berger Commission) working with the indigenous populations in Canada regarding the effects of a MacKenzie Valley Pipeline proposal in the 1970s[62]—is instructive in that it
did empower peoples normally excluded from the decision-making
process.[f] Berger literally transported the Commission's hearings to
the indigenous venues and reported back on their sentiments. In the
words of Mr. Justice Berger:

> No academic treatise or discussion, formal presentations of the
> claims of native people by native organizations and their leaders,
> could offer as compelling and vivid a picture of goals and aspira-
> tions of native people as their own testimony. In no other way could
> we have discovered the depth of feeling regarding past wrongs and
> future hopes, and the determination of native people to assert their
> collective identity today and in the years to come.[63]

However, the two Berger Commissions are prone to being seen as
anomalous examples and, more to the point, there are too few cor-
roborating instances.

Even sympathizers like Bobrow and Dryzek reach a similarly
frustrated conclusion: "Critical theory is dismissed by its opponents—and some of its friends—as irrelevant and abstract theoriz-
ing: the ideal speech situation is believed to be an unattainable construct."[64] To claim that the present administrative constructs are
more harmful than they should be (as most will at least partially admit) is not to demonstrate the contrary, that an alternative set of
procedures or conceptualizations is automatically superior, even if it
does appear more "democratic" in nature. John Forester addresses
the realistic point when he poses a legitimate, rather likely scenario:

> To the critical theorist who argues that truly democratic politics
> would solve the analyst's problems, or that the correction of ideo-
> logical distortions of communication could solve policy problems,
> the [traditional] analyst asks simply, "How? How will you 'democ-
> ratize' the state's agencies and all of the economy as well? Where's
> the experience that shows this can be done? Do you even have an
> articulate democratic theory of administration? A notion of 'democ-
> ratizing' (replacing?) large-scale bureaucracies? Show me![65]

---

[f]A second commission chaired by Mr. Justice Berger in the 1980s examined
the results of the 1971 Settlement Act for Alaskan indigenous peoples.

The forthright answer, as we saw earlier with hermeneutics and value-critical analysis, must be negative. But immediate practicality is not necessarily the sole reason for examining critical theory. In our case, it presents a fundamental set of responses to "How does the passage and implementation of a particular policy immediately alter, reproduce, replace, or create anew elements of . . . mediating institutions and organizations?" More to the central proposition, how does critical theory potentially affect the democratic processes? "Here we need a theory, not of risk or rankings, but of conditions of action and discourse, debate and argument, and, in an overall sense, democratic voice."[66] If this is our endeavor, then critical theory as a theory has well-rewarded the democratic investigation.

In Review

The purpose of these discussions is not to uncover any heretofore overlooked theory or jewel of public policy or governance from faraway lands or epistemologies. Rather, it is to review briefly some of the newer social science orientations to see if their special emphases can shed light on questions relating to democratic governance. In the earlier chapters, we have seen that the American democratic ethos is implicitly under attack by any number of unintentional but nevertheless real antagonists, such as less-than-representative bureaucracies or politicians, interest group politics, and hyperpluralism. These are not necessarily mendacious forces determined to undermine the government, rather simply facing "things" as they are and acting accordingly. They combine to remove citizens from participating in governance in a tangible manner, who appears to be none-too-enthusiastic as it is, perhaps because they view themselves as the object of political condescension and dismissal. What, then, might we learn from postpositivism that could conceivably improve the perceived lot of democracy and the democratic citizenry?

Three ideas stand out, particularly in contrast to the standard benefit-cost, rational man model. The first is that individual values cannot be assumed away under an utilitarian umbrella or Pareto optimality, as Amitai Etzioni, among others, have made clear.[67] Douglas Amy makes the point that politicians see little rationale or cause to delegate questions of morality and ethics to policy analysts, but as Martin Rein and others make clear, policy research is impossible if one compartmentalizes fact from value or treats them differentially; indeed, to do so warps the very frame of the analysis and probably the results.[68] The second insight is gleaned from the hermeneutic school, namely, that there is a wide variety of possibly important interpretations (personal, consensual, symbolic, "factual," etc.) that can be of particular utility in the policy process. To preclude one might be to preclude the (possibly) essential key. This also implies a wider participatory (i.e., less representative) base, in order to achieve a wider range of personal visions and insights.

Critical theory provides a third set of ideas that posit a more democratic discourse. With its insistence on multiple and equally respected perspectives in both fact and value, Habermas's strictures point most directly to a participatory democracy. But, as Dryzek cautions, "participatory democracy of itself has an ambiguous potential. Without communicative rationality, it will only add to the burdens of complexity." However, "On the other hand, communicative rationality without open participation will remain hobbled by the vestiges of control by a privileged group, and hence a dominant instrumental rationality. . . ."[69] In addition, as Helen Ingram and Steven Ragthed Smith have suggested, public policy can—indeed should—have a distinct effect on the communicative infrastructure among citizens, so there are means by which communicative rationality can be implemented.[70]

Robert B. Denhardt and Frank Fischer summarize by bookending the opposing point of views and prognoses detailed in this chapter. Denhardt offers what appears to be an methodological dirge for the policy sciences:

> . . . policy analysis depends solely upon those "value-free" techniques common to mainstream social science, the results inevitably support the existing "facts" of political and administrative life, including existing patterns of control. . . . They cannot reach creatively or imaginatively past that which exists in the past or present; their only projections are those based on the extrapolation of prior events. . . . By limiting ourselves to the examination of "measurable facts" of public policies or the "manifest behavior" of organizational actions, we implicitly endorse the social conditions which have created those facts and those behaviors.[71]

Fischer, on the other hand, appears to be more sanguine in his assessment, especially in terms of the salutory effects of postpositivism on democratic ends, when he proposes that it

> is only to argue that if policy science should return to its original commitment to a policy science [of] democracy . . . the field should

take seriously these deeper political and epistemological implications of a participatory methodology.[72]

We can thus turn to the final chapter, one that tries to synthesize many of these concepts into an operational policy sciences of democracy.

5

THE POLICY SCIENCES OF DEMOCRACY:
"TWO ROADS DIVERGED . . ."

Democracy means government by discussion but it is only
effective if you can stop people talking.

Clement Attlee, Speech at Oxford, 14 June 1957

Introduction

By way of preview, let me summarize the four main points I have
presented in the preceding four chapters. First, Americans appear
to be deeply disturbed by the predominance of the seemingly endless
gridlock in U.S. politics. Their frustration is repeatedly manifested
in terms of public opinion polls, popular literatures, the growing
phenomenon of "bureaucrat bashing," low voter turnout at elections,
and term limitations for politicians themselves. (Perhaps, when politicians engage in these quarrels, it becomes even more a national
embarrassment, a case of the pot calling the kettle black.) Without
pushing the particulars of the phenomena, the disgruntlement could
even extend to the point of disparaging the democratic processes
themselves. The policy sciences, nominally established as "the policy
sciences of democracy," have done little to address and relieve those
sentiments.

Second, American democracy during the past two hundred years
has been portrayed as if it were based on the De Tocquevillean
model of more direct citizen participation, civil virtue, and voluntary
associations, but it usually eventuates in practice as if it were more

97

deeply rooted in a Madisonian model, one predicated on indirect representation, constantly contending factions, and institutional checks and balances. The result increasingly too often turns into political stalemate, usually found on the federal level but, on occasion, working its way down to the state and local governments. Authors ranging from Robert Dahl to Robert Putnam decry the loss of such binding societal vectors as social capital, a shared national identity, civic virtue, or republican standards, and wonder how and if they can be restored. The policy sciences, to date, have offered little promise to these conditions.

Third, as just noted, the day-to-day policy sciences (especially under the rubric of policy analysis) have largely abandoned their democratic charter defined by Harold Lasswell and adopted an expertise, whatever the discipline, based on positivism, "instrumental rationality," the "rationality project," and technocracy. In combination, they basically divorce or separate the analysts and their product from the affected clientele, that is, the citizenry. At this juncture, we are left with a normative analytic hollowness that the philosopher William Barrett called "the illusion of technique."[1] Analysts have largely neglected what Martin Rein has called value-critical analysis. Robert B. Denhardt described the situation when he observed that policy analysts too-typically apply

> technical rules to the solution of immediate problems. Under such circumstances, technical concerns would displace political and ethical concerns as the basis for public decision making, thereby transforming normative issues into technical problems. . . . What is perhaps most troubling . . . is the possibility that only those policies will be entertained which are amenable to solution through the standard techniques of positivist social science. . . . The result is a new consciousness in which the world is viewed in terms of technique.[2]

Fourth and last, we find that several of the alternative policy research models propose elements of what John S. Dryzek, in line with a hermeneutic concept and critical theory, has called a "discursive democracy."[3] While granted that some of these postpositivist ideas are more "radical" than others (by contemporary analytic standards) they all seem to favor a greater degree of what Dan Durning, Frank Fischer, and Peter deLeon have termed a "participatory policy analysis."[4] They all explicitly call for the open inclusion of a wider range of diversity of interests relevant to the situation at hand and a more direct form of representation. What is presently lacking is "proof" that these and similar proposals actually are effective in terms of "better" policy, or at least as effective as the approaches they are supposed to displace. As we shall now argue, this "proof" argument is a specious opposition, because the two approaches are supplementary rather than mutually exclusionary.

The purpose of this final chapter is to assemble these strands into somewhat of a finished—or, more realistically, a projected—tapestry. The final product is by no means an easy theoretical weave, for both intrinsic and extrinsic obstacles are imposing for legitimate reasons. The United States has unquestionably assembled an impressive historical record of participatory democracy falling prey to more indirect representative practices. As just explained, the sheer magnitude of the citizenry makes a literal adoption of "communicative competence" of a participatory model impossible, even if the pervasive demands of major interest groups and an emerging global economy were not pressing. Also, one needs to address the role of authority in a deliberative society, just as one must ask if Michael J. Sandel's view of "republicanism" runs untoward risks of unwanted government intervention; in other words, does a more direct electorate suggest a "politics without guarantees"? In brief, what should be a fair and balanced aspiration in terms of democratizing the policy sciences and, with them, the American body politic?

Finally, the ideas of postpositivism might be theoretically well and good, but on a more workaday basis, how does one determine these basic issues such as what procedures are relevant or who has standing, indeed, what do we even mean by standing (i.e., questions of criteria), without dismissing the entire idea of postpositivism and discursive democracy as academic twaddle? As Attlee's epigram at the beginning of the chapter indicates, how can one restrict the potential (or actuality) for limitless prattle and posturing—that is, how can we reduce the likelihood of the standard criticism of the policy sciences, the infamous paralysis of analysis?—and still arrive at a manageable, discursive policy paradigm? Again, then, what can we present as an expected series of operational guidelines for a participatory policy sciences that honor the democratic conditions? Just as important, what might we argue that would persuade (if not convince) those who are skeptical of a postpositivist policy sciences?

We suggest, at least for the sake of the argument, a return to Leszek Kolakowski's (via Douglas Torgerson) metaphor of the priest and the jester. Let us with some confidence stipulate that the priesthood of the policy sciences is relatively well-entrenched in the academy, think tanks, and government offices. However, its abilities to address complex and important subjects (at least within the everyday bureaucracy) is often restricted to *supporting* or *supplementing* rather than *formulating* or *initiating* policy propositions. Moreover, as we have just seen, the analytic priesthood is doing little to discourage the ebbing of American's faith in government and, by extension, the democratic system, as it carries out its personal preferences, in procedure if not in specific programs. For these reasons, we might well implore the jester for policy guidance, as "a friend of openness, paradox, and diversity . . . [for] without the jester, [there is] no lively challenge for development."[5]

An American Democratic Dream

In chapter 2, we went to some lengths to spell out two differing dreams of the American democratic dream—one Madisonian, the other deTocquevillian, in their respective visions—and in how they have traced separate but unequal tracks throughout American history. The first offered an indirect, representative democracy, the second was more a function of civic associations and direct participation, with each interpreting itself as part of a series of historical precedents, movements, and philosophies. This argument does not try to resolve that particular dispute. What is does do, however, is contend that the Madisonian case and its continuation, while possibly the best mode for a long period of American history, does not—cannot—cope with the contemporary civic malaise and political frustration. It necessarily demands too much responsibility with too little accountability from the efforts of too few. Without totally abandoning the tenets of "old" democracy, we need to explore "new(er)" versions of democracy that focus on a greater respect and involvement of its members. Without these alternatives, we face little better than the status quo, and possibly (although unpredictably) worse.

This contention is much argued. Nancy L. Schwartz offers a careful comparison between the two democratic avenues and is sufficiently convinced to present the unequivocal statement "that political representation is qualitatively superior to direct democracy."[6] The original concern over the magnitude of the electorate has, of course, grown geometrically, to a place where, as Robert A. Dahl pointed out, a direct democracy for anything much greater than a town meeting (recall, he suggested an upper bound of six hundred persons) would be a logistic impossibility. Robert E. Goodin has addressed the problems suffered when a democracy must engage in what he calls "permissible paternalism," when, "For purposes of public policy, we think a person's more informed judgments command more respect than their less informed ones, their more settled judgments more respect than their less settled ones." Goodin cites addictive substances control as an example of the government exercising permissible paternalism, but other examples obviously become much more debatable (e.g., motorcycle helmets, OSHA regulations, or social welfare programs). Especially when "bundling" programs together to form coherent policies (as would be the case in social welfare policies), he elaborates that there is "reason to suppose that the preferences provoked by systems of indirect democracy such as 'democratic elitism' would be preferred by the people themselves on this score to those evoked by any system of direct democracy, even 'deliberative democracy.'"[7]

Nor does the promised advent of an "electronic democracy," made more feasible by electronic mail, two-way video- or telecommunications, or even some version of electronic voting, fulfill the direct democracy bill. Even (heroically) assuming universal access and capability to master the emerging technology, the complexity of contemporary public policy issues (to pick just two: sustainable development and Social Security) would make universal citizen involvement more time demanding than most would be willing (or able) to bear. There are additional questions of safeguarding confidentiality. Lastly, there is no reason to assume that the electronic voting rate would significantly rise, because we know that a democratic system is more than simply going to a polling station, as the high voting statistics (the highest among developed nations) but low governmental stability in Italy portend.[a]

The generic debate over who governs is not a new one in American politics. One of the most noted divisions over citizen versus elite democracy and "who should rule" was earlier this century, with Walter Lippmann publicly squaring off with John Dewey over the comparative merits of who should govern, the educated elites (Lippmann)

---

[a] A current poll sponsored by the League of Women Voters suggests that there is only one surefire variable predicting voter turn out—age. Seniors voting reach 68 percent, while those between 18 and 29 only attain 28 percent. Given the predicted demise of the senior-supporting Social Security system and its present-day funding by those younger, one wonders if this is not an electoral crisis in the making, a variation of a "minority-by-seniority" rule. Reported on National Public Radio's "Morning Edition," 1 July 1996.

or the people (Dewey). Lippmann, in *Public Opinion* (1922) and *The Phantom Public* (1925), claimed that the public's stake in governing themselves was more procedural than substantive, that the frontier's "omnipotent citizen" was yesteryear's (yesterday's?) anachronism, and that questions of vital public importance had to be decided by experts with valid information as opposed to the more visceral symbols that usually defined popular debates. In Lippmann's mind, the quality of information assuredly outweighed quantity. Christopher Lasch characterized Lippmann's fundamental position as one in which

> truth . . . grew out of disinterested scientific inquiry; everything else was ideology. The scope of public debate accordingly had to be severely restricted. At best public debate was a disagreeable necessity—not the very essence of democracy but its "primary defect." . . . Ideally public debate would not take place at all. . . .[8]

Dewey responded frontally in *The Public and Its Problems* (1927) by explaining how everyday discourse rather than scientific wisdom was the basis of the knowledge needed for a democratic governance. Dewey held that personal judgments and discursive interactions, augmented by public education, were the principal means for those achievements:

> The essential need . . . is the improvement of the methods and conditions of debate, discussion, and persuasion. That is *the* problem of the public. . . . It is not necessary that the many should have the knowledge and skill to carry on the needed investigations; what is required is that they have the ability to judge on the bearing of the knowledge supplied by others upon common concerns. . . . In its deepest and richest sense a community must always remain a matter of face-to-face intercourse. . . . Logic in its fulfillment recurs to the primitive sense of the word: dialogue.[9]

Unfortunately, the proper response was (or is) hardly transparent. If it were, solutions would have resolved political differences years and campaigns ago. For instance, many observers have thought that modern public survey techniques would offer a collective, social science salve. However, even as sage a polling analyst as Sidney Verba emphasizes that while "democracy implies responsiveness," and while scientific polling is surely valuable, polling cannot substitute for political participation or democratic processes. There are too many intervening, unspoken variables between the question and the ballot, including whether one will even use the ballot given the greater convenience of the polling question. Verba tells us that "The processes by which participants are selected are fundamentally different in the controlled world of the social survey and the real world of political participation. . . . Real life is dominated by selection bias."[10] Thus, he reduces surveys to little more than a scientific collection of data, usually more dependent upon the questioner than the respondent. While they are unquestionably important, surveys remain far from the political answer, for politics is far from being a science.

These judgments are offered *prior* to the initiation of anything resembling Jürgen Habermas's communicative rationality or unlocking hermeneutic circles, and the difficulties and uncertainties they might engender. In the face of *those* uncertainties, perhaps we should continue in our "muddling through," positivist manners. It is a fair enough question, because even if the results are mixed, the process is at least a well-established known.

At the same time, however, it should be clear that the "same old" is not paying the democratic bills. Books like E. J. Dionne's *Why Americans Hate Politics* and William Greider's *Who Shall Tell the People: The Betrayal of American Democracy* mirror, perhaps magnify the popular disgruntlement with the American political affairs. Academic reputations resonating these sentiments are being posed by, among others, Michael J. Sandel's *Democracy's Discontents: America in Search of a Public Philosophy* or Christopher Lasch's *Revolt of the Elites and the Betrayal of Democracy.*[11] While these books certainly are not contributory, they do indicate a growing discontent, as do the poor voter turnout and third-party candidacies. The public pollster Daniel Yankelovich links many of these trends together when he proposes that

> a new cultural value is respect for the public's clamor to participate in shaping the decisions that affect people's lives. Americans are increasingly unwilling to accept the traditional constraints of representative democracy whereby their representatives make the key decisions, and then in theory the public holds them accountable through the electoral process. All too often, this remote form of accountability does not work. People crave a more direct say in truly important policies, especially if such policies demand sacrifice.[12]

One could, of course, respond that these criticisms are little more than rhetoric and, to be sure, not very inflammatory at that. Moreover, why, one asks, would Americans wish to expand the voter lists to usher in the "vandals at the gate," in other words, to encourage "extremist" groups of every political hue and leaning to participate in a democratic system; why not leave them to simmer slowly in their own venom, unable to mount a working majority or coalition?

There are several responses to a quiet acceptance of this status quo. First, as matters presently stand, some extremist groups are already active in politics; it is the "sensible center" and the young who avoid the voting booths.[b] Second, some of the extremist groups adopt their peculiar stance because they see the American democratic system as completely insensitive and unresponsive; as such, they engage in a self-fulfilling but still-maddening prophecy. Third, and most important, there should—must—be a forum (or a series of fora) in which *all* voices and inclinations are recognized. The American dedication to political equality forces such a stance. The labor movements were publicly reviled in the United States during the last part of the nineteenth century, as were black Americans in many regions until more recently, but today they (and many others) are a legitimate, integral part of the American political system. Similarly, Hispanics have moved from a largely exploited minority to one actively wooed by political and commercial interests. Dewey spoke to the constant necessity to open the polity to challenge and alteration when he explained that "conditions of action and of inquiry and knowledge are always changing, the experiment must always be retried; the State must always be rediscovered."[13]

A number of worthwhile schemes have been put forth to expand American participation levels, such as "motor-voter" registration (in which a citizen can simultaneously obtain a driver's license and a voter's registration). One of the most interesting proposals was that of a "deliberative opinion poll" initially fashioned by James S. Fishkin. In his words,

> Deliberative opinion polls offer a new kind of democracy, one that combines deliberation and political equality. A deliberative opinion poll gives to a microcosm of the entire nation the opportunities for thoughtful interaction and opinion formation that are nominally restricted to small-group democracy. . . . It provides a statistical model of what the electorate *would* think if, hypothetically, all voters had the same opportunities that are offered to the sample in the deliberative opinion poll.[14]

---

[b]This League of Women Voters' survey also found that one-third of those self-identified as liberals voted, as compared to one-half of those self-identified as conservative.

Fishkin has proposed a type of national issues convention, with participants chosen by random lot, whose conferees would deliberate important issues of the day. More to our point, with the cooperation of the Public Broadcasting Service and National Public Radio, such a convention was held with 459 participants (600 were invited) in January 1996, in Austin, Texas, to discuss three issues of national standing—the economy, the state of the family, and America's role in the post-Cold War world. Sessions included a certain amount of educational activities and national political parties were invited to send their candidates. The results, while possibly illustrative, were limited by the obvious fact that this was a one-shot convention, with little chance for the participants to learn, reflect, and reprocess. Nor was there any indication that the convention was taken as seriously as its proponents would have preferred. But, more critically, not many minds were persuaded to new preferences and political positions. Surveys of the participants discovered that,

> Of the 81 questions answered before and then after the deliberative sessions, opinions on 61 questions were essentially unchanged. There were statistically significant changes on 20 questions. But in 13 instances respondents expressed more conviction about a position they held prior to deliberation. On only seven issues the balance of opinion changed. . . . [Basically, the] changes were dwarfed by the amount of stability in attitudes observed after the Austin convention.

Notably, views on such issues as opposing federal cuts in Medicare spending, reducing foreign aid, and opposition to NAFTA proved to be particularly resilient to change.[15]

In sum, the evidence at hand concerning the viability of an expanded democracy is admittedly circumstantial but worth summarizing: at least part of the current political discontent enveloping the American citizenry and nation is due to the continuing shortcomings of the representative brand of American politics, which basically ascribes to Madison's indirect democracy of checks and balances. Apparently Madison's genius failed to foresee that contending parties could be just as moderating—or gridlocking—an influence as his three prescribed branches of government. Likewise, the policy sciences, typically practiced in a conservative, marginalist manner, are doing little to remedy or even recognize the situation. Although it is beyond the purposes of this book to deal with the totality of the American democratic system, let us now turn our close attention to a critical theory of the policy sciences to examine what proposals it might offer to a policy science of democracy, in other words, to make it more attentive to this democratic roadblock.

The Critical Policy Sciences

The first task facing a critical policy sciences must be to incorporate some of the postpositivist concepts into modern policy research, both in terms of revealing something about the operations of the implementing bureaucracies and in making the research itself more responsive to its intended clients. The purpose is not to dictate public policy—a "gushing up" of policy preferences, if you will—but to assure that public sentiments are accurately accredited in policy-making circles in ways not synonymous with present-day interest group representations, public hearings, anecdotal information, or public opinion polls.

Regarding the first, Denhardt makes the point that

> Specifically, a critical theory of public organizations would (1) examine the technical basis of bureaucratic domination and the ideological justification for this condition and (2) ask in what ways members and clients of public bureaucracies might better understand the resultant limitations placed upon them by their actions and, in turn, develop new modes of administrative praxis.[16]

Denhardt continues to list the potential advantages of a critical theory paradigm for public organizations, pointing out how a discursive approach would have a therapeutic value within the bureaucracy by insisting "on highlighting those aspects of bureaucratic theory and practice which serve to limit the individual's recognition of and contribution to the process of governing." Similarly, it would be effectively diagnostic in emphasizing "the conditions of power and dependence which characterize contemporary organizational life and the considerable potential for conflict and disorder which these conditions portend. . . ."[17]

It is difficult to overstate Denhardt's attention to "breaking through the bureaucracy," as Michael Barzelay puts it,[18] because, not surprisingly, there is hardly any reason to assume that "advantaged" parties (e.g., present-day bureaucracies and interest groups) will surrender their advantage for the sake of a putatively level playing field for all the involved parties, or what Habermas has called "communicative competence." John Forester almost strikes a revolutionary pose when he suggests that "In the context of a technocratic or bureaucratic state, indeed, the call for democratization, for creating the conditions of open political discourse, for rational argument and criticism—this becomes a call for subversion of anti-democratic structures of investment and control" and would be viewed administratively as such.[19] Therefore, a concrete appreciation for the problematic assumptions inherent in critical theory on the institutional level—those of competent communicative actions, more diverse audiences, and particularly the reduction in "systematically communicative biases" (as opposed to an "ideal speech situation")—is necessary to avoid yet another round of shattered promises. The creation of rewards for institutional incentive structures moving toward more inclusive approaches are crucial for the success of a revived policy sciences.

While organizations are undoubtedly important, the key arena deals with the attention of, and attraction to, the individual citizen, who similarly needs to be persuaded that the critical policy sciences can operate in her or his best "interest," that it pays to become involved in the political system or else risk continued alienation and discouragement. This orientation is the linear stepchild of De Tocqueville's civic virtue, and a reiteration of authors like Carole Pateman and Jane J. Mansbridge who argued at length that a direct democracy was a more fulfilling democracy in terms of citizens' goals, not so much in their actual attainment of consensus or a strong economy but at least for their general understanding. Harold D. Lasswell made much the same claim for the policy sciences when, he, according to Torgerson,

> envisioned a profession which would promote both the general enlightenment of the population and the widespread sharing of power in a democratic policy process. What we witness in the development of Lasswell's work, then, is a methodological-political convergence which centers on *participation*. . . . Just as positivism underlies the dominant technical orientation in policy analysis, so the postpositivism orientation now points to a participatory project.[20]

Lasswell's emphasis on citizen participation is essential for it clearly indicates what "type" of democracy is required if these various recommendations for a renewed policy sciences are to be effective. To the point, a De Tocquevillian, participatory democracy—one featuring extended individual involvement leading to a more generalized political commitment—must be considered. This does not preclude the more usual Madisonian version from some roles and situations, but it is crucial that De Tocquevillean democracy (and its subsequent proponents) must be given their respective day in analytic court. This more participatory democratic orientation would imply two important transitions, one conceptual, the other on a more personal, participatory basis.

Conceptually, the critical policy sciences must relinquish their elaborately constructed aura of expertise or, put another way, the reluctance to include lay citizens in apparently technical and tightly structured policy deliberations. One means by which the necessary enthusiasm can be generated is the perspective that experts no longer rule the policy roost. As Ronald D. Brunner and William Ascher state, "science, as knowledge of fundamental principles of nature, is not a prerequisite for ameliorating particular policy problems nor are experts in command of such knowledge the only qualified participants in the policy process." Few recent phenomena manifest this more perfectly than the unorganized but prevalent "NIMBY" (Not in My Back Yard) sentiment used to counter many environmentally problematic projects.

Undoubtedly there is a legitimate avenue for increased and meaningful communications between existing authority and what Richard Rose calls *Ordinary People in Public Policy*. Rose pointedly warns that "Attention must be given to the use that ordinary people make of the programs produced by governments. . . . [That is], in a behavioral analysis, we need to think of public policy as inputs to the lives of ordinary people." Charles E. Lindblom succinctly restates the proposition: public policy should, "Instead of serving the needs of officials alone, help for the ordinary man."[21]

But making the plea does not make the case. There are new dynamics to encounter from critical theory, most of which are practically worrisome. We have already seen that public participation is not an alloyed benefit. Political theorists, in the United States as far back as the Founding Fathers (and before), have warned of the dangers of widespread public involvement, including mob psychology and the suppression of minorities and minority rights. In Michael J. Sandel's cautionary words, "Republican politics is risky politics, a politics without guarantees,"[22] as to where they will go and how they will get there. Where critical theory comes into direct play in the development of the critical policy sciences is the need to advance the communications process involved toward an open communicative ideal or, according to Davis B. Bobrow and John S. Dryzek, probably more realistically, "the analyst should work to eliminate systematically distorted communications" through a series of multiple perspectives, an equalization of capacities, and institutional innovations.[23] John Forester ties the package together by noting that critical theory helps frame the central dilemma by examining "the most difficult problem to which a critical theory of public policy leads: assessing citizens' recourse to scientific and political discourses—and the condition of power and systematic distortions that influence any effective resource and voice."[24]

While these areas of policy inquiry are nominally unchartered, some work in urban planning theory has been carried out that reflects well on the underlying beneficial nature of a critical theory approach in such programs as the "Healthy Cities" activities, advocacy planning, and "transactive planning." Urban planners as a matter of custom hold extensive and often informal meetings with residents in areas projected for urban renewal programs; for instance, it was discovered in one set of meetings that too often public parks, with their emphasis on football fields, basketball courts, and baseball diamonds, ignored the recreational needs of girls and women. Robert Hart explains that "advocacy planning means speaking for those who will actually use the buildings instead of doing research about them for those who hold the power. . . . It means helping people in a community do their own planning."[25] Melvin M. Webber once described this approach as a "different paradigm for planning," one in which "Its special task would then be to help assure that all parties' voices are heard. . . . [Thus,] the planner's role is as a facilitator of debate rather than as substantive expert."[26] Patsy Healy supports critical thinking in planning when she adds that "We cannot . . . predefine a set of tasks which planning must address, since these must be specifically discovered, learned about, and understood through intercommunicative processes."[27] John Friedmann refers to this approach as "transactive planning, one that "implies that we must find a way to join scientific and technical intelligence with personal knowledge at the critical points for social intervention." Like Robert A. Dahl, Friedmann emphasizes that there are times and places where transactive planning is inappropriate, *"where expertise carries sufficient authority to act without the benefit of mutual learning,"* such as the airline pilot or surgeon.[28] Unfortunately, Friedmann does not delineate these occasions, which, in practice, is preferable rather than a rockbound protocol too easy to quietly overlook or ignore.

Again, John Forester brings planning policy foursquare into critical theory when he comments that

> the responsibility of planning analysts is *not* to work towards the impossible perfection of "fully open communications." It is to work instead towards the correction of the *needless* distortions, some systematic and some not, that disable, mystify, distract, and mislead others: to work towards a political democratization of daily communications.[29]

We are clearly not suggesting that Habermas's or critical or hermeneutic thinking should be employed wholesale to public planning or policy. Nor are we proposing a vehicle for radical change. Our best reading of a generalized American public statement finds it rather homoestatic, one typically preferring stability, with marginal as opposed to revolutionary change. This view is substantiated by surveys taken this year during Fishkin's deliberative democracy experiment, in which the vast majority of opinions went unchanged.

Still, it is instructive to understand how certain ideas—especially Habermas's proscription toward at least a more commonly held "communicative competence"—fit rather comfortably into a revised policy sciences and indicate what adjustments might be useful. We know, for instance, that the composition of panels can make a very large difference in their panels' findings, even in relatively technical areas such as medical research, as a recent study from the National Institute of Health confirmed.[30] Rather, it is more important to realize the potential advantages of a critical policy sciences for the public organizations as a whole and how they interact on a practical basis with its citizens. Denhardt addresses these issues:

> [A] critical approach would insist on highlighting those aspects of bureaucratic theory and practice which serve to limit the individual's recognition of and contribution to the process of governing. . . . [A] critical approach would emphasize the conditions of power and dependence which characterize contemporary organizational life and the considerable potential for conflict and disorder which these conditions portend. . . . Moreover, . . . by specifying the ways in which current relationships of power and dependence result in alienation and estrangement, a critical theory of public organizations would suggest more direct attempts to improve the quality of organizational life.[31]

There is, of course, no ironclad guarantee that the proposed organizational setup will produce "better" public policy or that its derived programs will always "solve" pressing social problems. Most policy problems are far too complicated to warrant any such confidence. As just noted, public policymakers themselves might object, sensing more a loss of authority than the benefits of a more informed policy decision. Lastly, public sector organizations would almost surely find the critical thinking philosophy and procedures anathema to their existing operating procedures and power relationships, and therefore pose significant obstacles to their adoption. Yet, we can justifiably ask if the jester is not on to the germ of a valuable idea, for the very arguments against a critical policy sciences are most often couched from its strongest opponents (i.e., those with the most to lose), mostly framed in procedural rather than substantive criticisms.

Participatory Policy Analysis

We now turn toward a more individual oriented aspect of a critical policy sciences methodology, one a number of policy researchers have characterized as "participatory policy analysis." Dan Durning has reviewed four versions of participatory policy analysis (PPA) and found that they shared a number of common features, specifically: "All reject positivism; view phenomenology or a variation of it, as a better way to interpret the nature of knowledge; and accept an interpretative or hermeneutic paradigm of inquiry."[32]

Fundamentally, the idea behind PPA is that more-generalized and less-vested panels composed of citizens at large are empowered to participate in deliberations over public policy issues over an extended period of time (say, a year). A participatory policy analysis methodology would require policy analysts to select Rose's "ordinary citizens," randomly chosen from a broadly defined pool of affected citizens (possibly formulated to take sociocultural variables into account) so as to avoid the stigma of being "captured" by established interests and stakeholders, to engage in a participatory analytic exercise.[33] Ortwin Renn and his coauthors state that the objective of PPA, in their words, is to

> provide citizens with the opportunity to learn about the technical and political facets of policy options and to enable them to discuss and evaluate these options and their likely consequences according to their own set of values and preferences. . . . In contrast of negotiations with stakeholder groups, our model of participation is inspired by the normative goal of a fair and impartial representation of all citizens' values and preferences, be they organized or not.[34]

The extended tenure of a PPA panel is important because it allows a panel to gain particular knowledge in the subject area as well as becoming socialized to one another. A longer tenure could help overcome the limitations earlier ascribed to Fishkin's idea of a temporary forum of deliberative democracy.

The PPA concept of citizen participation is analogous to that of a jury, a parallel also drawn by Fishkin, when he writes that "both are meant, in one sense, to be representative of ordinary citizens. Both are premised on the notion that ordinary citizens, when immersed in the relevant materials, can deal with difficult intellectual questions."[35] In this sense, he offers a direct comparison to the citizen juries under the classical Athenian democracies, one that places real faith in citizens' abilities to "work through a problem," even if staff support is required or occasional errors are made. Dahl makes a similar proposal when he talks about a "minipopulous" or citizen assemblies. Suppose, says Dahl, that

> an advanced democratic country were to create a "minipopulous" consisting of perhaps a thousand citizens randomly selected out of the entire demos. Its task would be to deliberate, for a year perhaps, on an issue and then to announce its decision. . . . The judgment of a minipopulous would "represent" the judgment of the demos.[36]

The jury concept is far from an exact parallel. The citizen juries do not, for instance, *determine* policy, like a jury in a criminal trial; rather, they are designed to "advise" the policymakers. Their deliberations should not be closed nor necessarily confidential. Unlike a jury, they require support staff and invariably a relatively unbiased education into the issues at hand (although some would claim that the adversarial presentations in the court serve a didactic purpose, though one can doubt their balance). Nor, like politics, are they above bias or prejudice. These distinctions do not mean that they strictly hypothetical. Dahl and Fishkin both report on the work of Ned Crosby and the Jefferson Center for New Democratic Processes in Minnesota, which for years have been active in deliberating local policies, such as the effect of agriculture on water policy or the ethics of organ transplantation, with panels of about a dozen citizens.[37]

More germane to the PPA brief is the example in Boulder, Colorado, where Lyn Kathlene and John A. Martin explained how a citizen panel (of approximately one-hundred-fifty participants), sitting for over a year, assisted Boulder city officials in planning a new transportation grid for its metropolitan bus service, which would qualify for a complex task in most people's book. Their findings are encouraging for a PPA proposal, as they concluded that

> Citizen panels can provide a workable alternative to other, perhaps more traditional, citizen participation techniques. The citizen information panel combines statistically representative sample selection, and survey and interview techniques, with "timeliness" and relevance to create large, active, and informed community-wide source of planning information and policy preference opinion. . . . And panels enable planners and policy makers to better understand the community they serve.[38]

The deliberative or discursive panel would be designed to address a single, specified policy issue. For particular complex issues addressing large state or federal problems, there is no reason why a series of panels could not be created to both enhance the diversity of perspectives as well as capturing regional variations; air pollution, grazing lands, water rights, or acid rain would be likely examples. Thus, a number of groups could be simultaneously empaneled. Since the panels are advisory in nature, there is no reason for them to be competitive or played off against one another; their declared purpose would be to give better information, not better solutions.

A designated team of policy analysts from the relevant government agencies could present a certain amount of agreed-upon material to the groups, including the contrary positions, in such a manner as to educate these people to the directions and magnitudes of the given issue. Agency (or multiple agencies') analysts would also provide the necessary staff support, basically organizing meetings and communications but possibly setting up and implementing electronic communication links. Lastly, a framework regarding discursive protocols would need to be established and monitored for both the regular exchanges as well as for formal panel meetings. While none of these procedures would be tamperproof, in these ways selected participants would serve as a representative and informed citizenry without having the potentially onerous baggage now attributed to interest groups and individuals who typically testify to various legislative and regulatory hearings.

As Dewey and others have observed, an educative feature of the panels would be an important element of the panels' deliberations. There is little doubt that the complexities underlying many public policy deliberations—currently held mostly among "experts" —are more detailed and complicated than the layperson would ordinarily know. In lieu of salient knowledge, undereducated guesses, even hunches, could become the unfortunate rule of thumb. Therefore, pedagogical functions are imperative, both for the policy itself and for the participants' self-confidence that they are making thoroughly, thoughtfully informed choices, as is the case with jury deliberations.

Take, for instance, the question of how much foreign aid the United States should offer, which a poll released by the Program on International Policy Attitudes at the University of Virginia surveyed. The results found that 75 percent of Americans thought that the United States spent too much on foreign aid and 64 percent wanted foreign aid spending cut. Respondents were then asked what was the level or the current proportion of U.S. foreign aid in the federal budget; the median answer was 15 percent; the average answer was 18 percent. The proposed median reduction was reduced down to 5 percent, with an average of 3 percent being considered "too little." Of course, the U.S. government spends a little less than 1 percent of its budget on foreign aid.[39]

Policy panels must have access to a certain amount of agreed-upon information, or at least accepted ranges of such information, if they are to be able to find some levels of consensual advice. Again, the principal burden of this information requirement should primarily be assumed by the policy staff, with safeguards being taken to assume a balanced assessment, if not always (ever?) a consensual one. Likewise, the lack of agreement with the panels is one of the genuine strengths of the policy forum—it need not issue a unanimous finding, like a criminal jury; it can be quite content to report a mixed set of policy readings, for its virtue is not to dictate to a government agency or policymaker, but rather to make sure that they are well informed as to what constituents think and maybe even feel.

Since the PPA exercises would be carried out over periods largely determined by some combination of issue parameters (especially timing) and the participants' schedules and commitment, it would be incumbent upon the PPA analytic staff to understand the panel members' possibly competing priorities and to make adjustments to conform to their schedules. For these reasons, analysts would need to be persuasive in their efforts to recruit and *maintain* the policy panel to ensure a continuity. Citizens would probably have to be compensated for their involvement, both in financial remuneration and work release measures, in line with James S. Coleman's statements of "social capital." However, the main attraction—the necessary motivation (once more akin to jury duty)—would ultimately be the perceived importance of civic participation or what De Tocqueville called the civil community.

The linchpin inducement to the citizen/participant, therefore, would be the knowledge that their efforts would be assured a careful, considered hearing in the policy-making process, that is, their deliberations would not constitute a charade, a sham of citizen participation. Kathlene and Martin conclude in their review of citizen participation that, "In determining whether or not participation will have a positive payoff, people take into account the time involved, the importance of the issue, their own personal knowledge and competence regarding the issue, and the likelihood that their opinions will make a difference."[40] In other words, before citizens can be expected to invest in *their* social capital regarding the policy process, they must realize that *it* is investing in them (hence, the need for nominal compensation) and respects their discursive activities, sacrifice, and advice.

As the discursive panels attained a level of competence in the subject matter, these fora—what we might choose to call a "policy forum"—would begin to approximate the second feature of a post-positivism critical policy analysis, the environment for (if not the fact of) supporting Habermas's communicative rationality. The policy forum purpose and proceedings would build upon the work of Hank C. Jenkins-Smith who outlined what he labeled the "analytic fora." Jenkins-Smith elaborated the important distinction between open and closed meetings. The open meeting included "all mobilized participants within the subsystem . . . [and is characterized by] the lack of shared norms of scientific investigations and resolution of competing empirical claims." While the open forum moves toward the desired democratic ethos, its diversity and resulting inherent lack of boundaries suffer from too many views and voices, such that "analysis can be expected to back many sides of the debate, and generally will not provide a basis for consensus. . . ."[41] The open forum would be democratic but anarchic.

The closed forum participant, on the other hand, is more likely to share some of these norms toward great consensus, because its members have been preselected on given common criteria, such as a prior knowledge base. However and concomitantly, its closed, restrictive discourse would naturally exclude a wider range of experiences and values, that is, to limit the variegated views of democracy that underlies the critical policy sciences' theory. Compared to the open forum, it would be orderly but not democratic.

The suggestion here is to develop a much more proactive policy forum procedure, in which participants are chosen by lot to serve on a representative basis (i.e., a open policy forum) and then educated to the intricacies of the policy arguments at hand (a closed forum). In this manner, the panel members can share a certain body of information and procedures while being receptive to a wider degree of citizen representation. The policy forum produces a variation of Jenkins-Smith's preferred "professional forum," one that is more likely to reach an informed consensus than the cacophony of the open forum and more likely to manifest consensual democratic values than the closed forum. One should never hope to eliminate completely all the vestiges of advantage (in Habermasian terms, to replace implicit communication asymmetries with communicative competence); some "silver-tongued devils" would always have an edge over the more reticent speaker. That is the price direct democracy extracts. However, the policy forum concept would be designed to move in this more discursive direction.

In support of the policy forum idea, many scientists and citizens alike are currently realizing that the most "technical" decisions in the public sector are, at heart, political, thereby agreeing with Brunner and Ascher and further undermining the technologist's claim to exclusive participation or layperson exclusion, and likely to become undemocratic in nature. Renn and his colleagues flatly observed from their studies that "Technocratic decision making is incompatible with democratic ideals."[42] John Bridger Robinson makes an excellent case as to the technical shortcomings of many sophisticated methodologies such as risk analysis and energy forecasting. He argues that if their technical powers for policy advice are inherently limited in insight and predictive capabilities, then their proponents' reluctance to involve laypersons lacks support, indeed becomes untenable, as a spurious instance of technological determinism and value-free analysis. Robinson continues to explain how the important transition would reflect

> the attempt to develop a new concept of science, one that is more integrated into the policy context, more contextual and openly value-laden, less oriented to mastery over natural and social processes, and more accessible to the public at large. . . . The focus therefore shifts from keeping mandated science pristine and free of

the policy process (which allows its continued hidden use as legitimation for policy decisions made for other reasons) to developing a means by which it can be more strongly integrated into that process and recognized to be providing only a limited, and somewhat conditional, part of the answer.[43]

Fortunately, there is an accumulating body of evidence that citizens are generally willing to engage in civil activities that approach these conditions in a spirit of personal morality and civic responsibility that transcends strict economic self-interest and compensation.[44] One of the lessons from Fishkin's Austin National Issues Convention was a willingness to commit to these sorts of responsibilities for a perceived public good, and that "the average participant expressed more sympathetic views" for their coparticipants' opinions whom they normally would not have met. Moreover, there are some data reflecting a "spillover" effect between citizen involvement and democracy that De Tocqueville would have predicted, that is, "where people feel connected," voter participation improves markedly.[45]

In support of the more participatory position, there is a growing number of studies that suggest that citizens can, if they wish, become well-informed and pivotal discussants. Paul A. Sabatier and Anne M. Brasher's long-term study of the Lake Tahoe environmental disputes and resolution richly illustrates this capability for citizen/expert involvement as a policy-learning experience.[46] Frank Fischer cites two environmentally oriented cases in his PPA examples of citizens exercising the NIMBY reservation for projects designed to be built in their neighborhoods.[47] Likewise, where schools are being decentralized back to neighborhoods, one finds a similar level of local participation.

In a comparative study, Renn and his colleagues describe two cases of public participation (in the Federal Republic of Germany and in the State of New Jersey) in a very structured decision-making environment, one they call "Citizen Panels for Policy Evaluation and Recommendations." In their research design,

> the objective is to provide citizens with the opportunity to learn about the technical and political facets of policy options and to enable them to discuss and evaluate these options and their likely consequences according to their own set of values and preferences.[48]

Their findings were guardedly positive, leading to the "systematic combination of professional expertise, social interests, and public values for selecting and evaluating policies."[49] An encouraging finding from our standpoint by Renn (at least in the New Jersey experiment) was that the panelists were often not content to be "handed" materials by the experts, but chose to subject them to critical analysis, thus further substantiating the discursive capabilities of citizens and their panels.

In their award-winning analysis of the processes characterizing urban democracy, Jeffrey M. Berry and his colleagues reviewed fifteen community redevelopment programs in midsize American cities and found superior results in terms of governance among those cities that had the greater degree of administrative "outreach" and reciprocal local citizen involvement. The authors initially complained that

> government officials . . . can rationalize that there is no reason to build a substantive citizen participation structure because public involve programs do not work. . . . [Moreover] Unfortunately social scientists have largely given up on participatory democracy. . . . [But] The data here show that when administrators make a good-faith effort to make citizen participation work rather than trying to undermine it, the performance of public involvement programs is dramatically different from that described in the literature.[50]

Their conclusions are naturally guarded (this is, after all, social science), but like Renn and his colleagues, Berry and his coauthors are quite positive, especially given that they are working on a much broader scale:

> In general, increased participation does lead to greater sense of community, increased governmental legitimacy, and enhanced status of governmental institutions. In general, the fears that expanded participation efforts will engender rising and unmet expectations or promotion of antidemocratic or antisystem attitudes are unfounded. . . . Even though participants do not get everything they seek, they feel that government is listening to what they have to say. This feeling is strengthened as participation becomes more frequent and consistent.[51]

To be fair, the evidence in the urban democracy arena is still mixed and one needs to exercise some reservations here, because a demand for local decentralization does not necessarily deliver what is expected, however pressing the need. In their analysis of urban politics, William E. Lyons and his colleagues demonstrate to the contrary, that decentralized political decision making does not always result in greater citizen knowledge of, participation in, or satisfaction with local government services.[52]

Some PPA critics claim that citizen organizations (particularly of the voluntary type) are inherently unable to channel constructively individual citizen involvements to public purposes. Although the number of "public service" nonprofit organizations is presently growing to astronomical numbers, the results possibly linking nonprofit associations to democratic behaviors are not yet in. Still others charge that local empowerment can empower the wrong people doing the wrong thing, with the latter being increasingly heard in the acrimonious battles for control of local school boards and education policies. But these contentions, while valid precautions, fail to acknowledge the public's wisdom in dealing responsibly *on its own terms of reference* with difficult community problems. Environmental, educational, health care issues, and nuclear disarmament are only four examples of issue areas in which citizen involvement has been shown to be reasoned and convincing.

Nor does an affirmation of open citizen participation and a discursive community orientation mean that all issues are equally suitable to this postpositivist mode of analysis and policy-making. Variations in conditions (e.g., time, dispersion, or magnitude) certainly require variations in perspective and means. What we find is another manifestation of contingency theory, or a simple acceptance of a basic tenet the policy sciences refer to as contextuality: a contingency theory insists that different contexts require different timelines, approaches, and resolutions. More concrete questions—such as who decides which parties have the relevant voices, the utilized criteria, or even what are the criteria—are daunting (especially for the hermeneutic analysis) but secondary for the moment to the more contextual acceptance of the participatory policy analysis approach.

Nevertheless, we can tailor these and similar postpositivist methodologies in a variety of policy-accommodating ways. They can be utilized in specific organizations and given contingencies in which their applications are more amenable or suitable. For instance, a strictly hierarchical institution (e.g., a Weberian bureaucracy, typically the military or police forces) with its particularized organizational ethics would be much less receptive to the critical policy sciences than an organization characterized by communitarian or network structures and ethics, as is the case with many of the proverbial street level bureaucrats (e.g., teachers or social workers). (As an aside, the police, who share the two traits, would be a fascinating test case.)

A second discriminating criterion would be the urgency or the secrecy attached to a policy decision. Even though crisis management (where uncertainty reigns in both ends and means) would necessarily violate the critical theory ground rules of nondistorted, nonhierarchical exchange, a genuine political crisis (e.g., the Cuban missile crisis, a nuclear power reactor disaster such as occurred at Three Mile Island, or the assassination of a prime minister) could not accept either the publicity or the time requirements demanded by PPA or policy fora. Natural disasters, such as floods or hurricanes, would also be time sensitive but could fit into a PPA format in preplanning for a generalized natural disaster.

On the more amenable other hand, a PPA examination of the health care delivery system, immigration, education reform, and other social welfare policies would be relatively less time intensive (although no less important) and therefore more suitable to these procedures.[53] Indeed, their present-day process through the existing channels of government is already glacial in pace (if not in effect). The environmental assessment process (as manifested by the environmental impact statement) originally thought to be excruciating time-consuming and debilitating, has today become an accepted (and, by many, a highly valued) part of the governing process. Likewise, decentralized management of public schooling is not famed for its expeditious ways but is still growing in popularity and has even extended its way into the charter schools movement. All of these might easily be receptive to a PPA under the guise of the critical policy sciences.

We cannot leave the issue of postpositivism without considering the role of authority, for authority is regularly left in the residual lurch. Authority is a topic that must be addressed for fear of an impending government by ceaseless deliberation but that does not fit easily into a postpositivist paradigm. Mark Warren makes the case that deliberative democracy *requires* an authority component because of its functional nature: there are too many decisions (some of which we have discussed do not lend themselves to a discursive approach) for a minipopulus or policy forum to consider. So, under a policy forum regime, a trusted authority is crucial for the everyday operations of government. Alternatively, Warren argues that a discursive democracy can help "align" or validate authority and thus establish the necessary trust that would allow policy fora to pay their limited attentions to more serious matters. Thus, he claims that democratic "authority involves a limited suspension of judgment enabled by a context of democratic challenge and public accountability."[54]

While Warren's argument has some validity, it is not especially pressing in the case of the critical policy sciences or PPA, for they are deliberately advisory—not governing—in nature. The reasoning is straightforward, going back to Lasswell: the policy sciences of democracy are to improve governance by providing better, more complete information, information that the policymakers can then put to good use. To endow citizen panels with genuine authority would be to undercut their representativeness to their fellow citizens, causing them to think that these panels have done little to the democratic processes except to change one elected group of distant authorities for a random group of now-even-less-accountable authorities, the latter with no visible means of recourse or recall. Furthermore, with authority comes the trappings of competitiveness, struggles over respective domains, and power struggles. In this sense, the policy fora are better off having a responsibility for representation rather than the often accompanying epithets concerning authority.

The final link in a postpositivist orientation deals, of course, with the training of the individual policy analyst. As Marie Danzinger has pointed out with particular clarity, present-day policy schools' curricula are hardly brimming with postpositivism, for reasons we can easily imagine.[55] If we know anything about the university, we know that it is rarely radical in its changes. But to incorporate the critical policy sciences, one would need to include new methodologies and skills for the budding (as well as the midcareer) policy analyst that would encourage such capabilities as being a mediator/facilitator (rather than a strict analyst), probably ethnography, some fields of sociology dealing with interviewing, survey research methods, and other postpositivist approaches.

There are also many discrete items one could propose to move from the Madison to the De Tocqueville version of the policy sciences. Public policies, for instance, could be devised that would explicitly urge participation of citizens;[56] in this instance, political power would have to be devolved to local levels so that citizens could see the results of their political and social experiments, thereby encouraging their continued involvement.[57] Public administrators would have to exchange their favored bureaucrat's tweeds (and mentalities) for educator's gowns, as well as review their agencies' goals and relationships from a critical perspective, as suggested by Robert Denhardt and others.[58] A more general sense of openness and community rather than oversight and isolation would be the order of the day.

Policy analysts would need to expand their arsenal of methodologies to learn to listen as well as analyze, which, as we know, is anything but straightforward. As Jane Aronson observed from recent experiences in Canada, participation in government deliberations has not been particularly successful, largely because of the ways in which the meetings were structured and conducted. She cautions against the respective "clash of vocabularies" (seniors literally did not understand the questions being asked by the analysts), the "existence of the present limits to the consultative process," and a general "disparity of power" between those interviewing and those being interviewed (e.g., being asked to pose alternative modes of delivery). Aronson concluded that "if the bolder, more democratizing aims of participation are to be realized, it is evident that professionals and administrators in service and planning organizations will be required to share power and control that has, typically, been concentrated within fairly hierarchical structures."[59] While easy to note, Aronson's suggestions would again raise several layers of bureaucratic hackles. Still, that is why we have jesters, for the rewards of moving ahead could easily overcome the priestly safety of remaining stationary.

"Two Roads Diverged in a Yellow Wood . . ."

We have presented a case, admittedly a provisional examination, explaining why and how the policy sciences can be more relevant to public policymakers and, more important, reclaim their overlooked democratic heritages. In the "why" case, we have emphasized how the policy sciences can recede from the perceived abyss of the "end of policy analysis" only half-facetiously prophesized by David L. Kirp,[60] elaborating on its more humanistic side.

We have observed that there are two avenues for the renewed policy sciences that must be traveled simultaneously—an institutional road enlightened by the lamp of postpositivism, and an individual commitment to civil virtue, also made clearer by postpositivism. Neither is easy nor automatic. In a skeptical review of postpositivism, Edward F. Lawlor asks "what separates the analyst from the journalist or consumer advocate under this new argumentative turn? What separates the policy analyst from literary theorist and critic in the case of narrative policy analyst?" Lawlor's assessments are not forgiving:

> To disconnect policy analysts from their disciplinary roots and
> charge them with the general communicative functions espoused
> by the new argumentative school would not only remove "tools" as a

defining feature of the field, it would further undermine the already shaky intellectual identity of the field. Postpositivism and so-called postmodernism in policy analysis is a swamp of ambiguity, relativism, and self-doubt . . . creating more problems for the policy analysis business than it solves.[61]

Lawlor is both wrong and right. He is "wrong" in that he equates the continuation of traditional policy analysis as an ongoing success story, hampered only by cynical politicians, ungrateful citizens, and carping postpositivist nay-sayers. But we have already seen how conventional policy analysis is less of a growth industry and more one fully prepared to recline on its marginalist laurels. And he is "wrong" in that he sees no ray of postpositivist revelation, thus returning the field to the relatively sterile world of benefit-cost analysis, stagnating a field strictly as a function of its tools; imagine any prospering discipline of inquiry using basically the tools of three decades ago. He is "right" in making the case that, inter alia, the critical policy sciences must set forth a menu of quality standards or risk indeed becoming "a swamp of ambiguity. . . ." While this is not simple in any—let alone a postpositivist—world, it provides a basis for product validity for the critical policy sciences.

While neither the institutional nor the individual path is easy, both are imperative. The first is essential, for it is through institutions that citizens can act to govern. The popular contemporary observations that the relevant administrative and legislative institutions are no longer accountable give rise to a sense of gridlock and resulting civic frustration. Perhaps, however, the reestablishment of an operational civil culture or a reaffirmation of social capital is the more difficult, for it requires commitment and sacrifice from a now-alienated citizenry. We have already seen how feminist politics fell short in their attempt to implement a more direct democracy. Still, a civic culture is the only way in which a democratic ethos (or an acceptable vision of one) can be reaffirmed. Jeffrey M. Berry and his colleagues conclude their study by noting that "Participatory democracy is offered by theorists as an alternative to representative democracy; in the real world, institutions for strong democracy must be integrated into a system that also includes institutions of representative democracy."[62] Political theorists ranging from Alexis De Tocqueville to John Dewey to Harold Lasswell (with many more in between) make much the same reinforcing proposal.

Former speaker of the House of Representatives, Tip O'Neill, is reputed to have said "that all politics is local." He was, of course, talking of the world of practical politics. However, the O'Neill maxim is assuredly the case for the integration of the policy sciences and democracy. We have found a number of supporting cases, all of which hinge on the concept of citizen participation, and their involvement on local levels of government. Here we have reiterated that duality as well as offering an initial framework for making such a transition between institutions and individuals in terms of a participatory policy analysis. Undoubtedly the framework for the proposed critical policy sciences needs to undergo serious revision—isn't that the very nature of postpositivism in any case?—but at least we are presenting a beginning, with the hope that it will not be an end.

If a critical policy analysis can reduce the syndrome of trying to compare the proverbial "apples to oranges" (or, as John Bridger Robinson graphically characterized the American energy debates, comparing "apples and horned toads"[63]), they will have made a major contribution. We are not arguing for a "sea change" in the policy sciences. Rather, we are pleading the worth—or, more honestly, the acceptance—of a contingency approach: for some everyday types of policy problems, a traditional risk or benefit-cost analysis might be perfectly appropriate. But for other, more complicated instances, we would propose at least the careful consideration of what we have articulated here to be the critical (some would say the emancipated) policy sciences.

If participatory policy analysis is taken seriously by citizens, analysts, and policymakers, it might very well extend to a revitalization of social capital and to what many observers have called a flagging faith in democracy and its governance. We have proposed here a means to reinvest citizens with what they perceive to be their democracy and its institutions. Even though more thoughtful analyses are readily welcomed, the reuniting of the policy sciences and democracy would undoubted be the most valued end result. We do not necessarily have to succeed, but we do need to try.

We began this final section with a line from Robert Frost's often-cited (but rarely, one suspects, in support of a postpositivist tract) "Road Not Taken," as a means of suggesting that this analysis is far from a finished product. Promising, one trusts, well-argued, one hopes, but hardly finished. Honoring symmetry, we conclude with the intention that the policy sciences might be viewed as having two roads of their own, the conventional and the critical, or, alternatively, a traditional but inherently elitist policy sciences and a more deliberative policy sciences of democracy. We have somewhat discouraged the case for the first (the bishop's miter) and encouraged an alternative case for the second (the jester's coxcomb), with Frost's beseeched blessing, who wrote eighty years ago that he or she or

> I shall be telling this with a sigh
> Somewhere ages and ages hence:
> Two roads diverged in a wood, and I—
> I took the one less traveled by,
> And that has made all the difference.

NOTES

Preface

1. Compare, for instance, Hank C. Jenkins-Smith (1990), who argues for the worrisome but not yet here phenomenon, with John S. Dryzek (1989), who is more pessimistic. Also see Frank Fischer (1990).

2. See Peter deLeon (1988) for a general statement to this effect even though in the past few years, the wider circulation of the policy sciences approach is easily distinguishable.

1. The Democratic Dream

1. Christopher Lasch (1995), pp. 1, 85.

2. Benjamin Barber (1984) is one of the most noted academic critics of American democracy as practiced; others include James S. Fishkin (1991). Lani Guinier (1994) proposes a number of remedies, particularly for minority voters.

3. E. J. Dionne (1991), p. 10.

4. Michael J. Sandel (1996), p. 1.

5. Compare Los Angeles Times-Mirror Center for the People and the Press Surveys, 8 December 1994, 11 January 1995, and 13 April 1995, and 13 May 1996. A parallel statistic was published by Kevin Phillips (1994): the decline in response to "How much of the time can you trust the government to do what's right?" went from 76 percent in 1964 to 19 percent in 1994.

6. Robert D. Putnam (1994) makes the case that while bowling has increased in numbers of participants (by 10 percent), there are fewer bowling

leagues (by 40 percent). While this might seem irrelevant, Putnam notes that some eighty million people bowled during 1993, "nearly a third more than voted in the 1994 Congressional elections." Also see Putnam (1995).

7. William Greider (1992), p. 11.

8. See P. deLeon (1993) for an account and possible explanation.

9. John Kenneth Galbraith (1996).

10. Fischer (1990).

11. Herbert Goldhamer (1978) has traced policy advice back through the millennia, while Arnold Meltsner (1990) describes policy advice as proffered to "rulers."

12. Harold D. Lasswell (1949a and 1949b). Quotation from Lasswell (1951), p. 15. Of course there were other major contributors, both in the United States (e.g., John Dewey [1927], Robert S. Lynd [1939], and Robert K. Merton [1936]), as well as major figures overseas (e.g., Karl Mannheim [1936]).

13. Irving Louis Horowitz (1981). Also see the memoirs of Reagan's director of the Office of Management and Budget, David Stockman (1985).

14. Alice M. Rivlin (1984), pp. 18–19.

15. This trait is made quite clear by Bob Woodward's (1994) discussion of the first year of the Clinton administration.

16. P. deLeon (1992), p. 126.

17. Dryzek (1989), p. 98.

18. James A. Morone (1990) has done a splendid job in tracing the development of the American democratic wish and its inherent difficulties. Also see Giovanni Sartori (1987).

19. Joshua Cohen and Joel Rogers (1981), p. 18.

20. Sandel (1996), chapter 9.

21. For instance, see the essays edited by Helen Ingram and Steven Ragthed Smith (1993), who argue that public policies should be specifically tailored to encourage democratic participation.

22. Aaron Wildavsky (1979), p. 5.

2. Visions of Democracy

1. A representative sampler of definitions and obfuscations is found in Carl Cohen (1971), Graeme Duncan (1983), and H. B. Mayo (1960). Cohen

(p. 21) illustrates the semantic confusion when he cites Hitler as referring to Nazism as "real" democracy and Mussolini describing Italian fascism as "an organized, centralized, and authoritarian democracy." Perhaps the most thorough explanation is found in Sartori (1987).

2. Sartori (1987), p. 6; emphasis in original.

3. Philippe Schmitter and Terry Lynn Karl (1991), p. 75.

4. Cohen (1971), p. 7.

5. Schmitter and Karl (1991), pp. 75, 76.

6. Nancy L. Schwartz (1988), p. 7.

7. Sartori (1987), p. 8.

8. One of the major strengths of Robert A. Dahl's *Preface to Democratic Theory* (1956) is his splendid analysis of both of these schools.

9. Sandel (1996), p. 5.

10. John Stuart Mill, in his 1835 introduction to the English edition of *Democracy in America*, made this comparison between Montesquieu and De Tocqueville: "The book [*Democracy in America*] is such as Montesquieu might have written, if to his genius he had superadded good sense. . . ." Mill (1961), p. xiv. Madison pays explicit homage to Montesquieu in *The Federalist Papers*, No. 47.

11. Richard W. Krouse (1983), p. 59.

12. Montesquieu's *Spirit of the Laws* is quoted in Fishkin (1991), pp. 15 and 16.

13. Madison's life and political philosophy are documented by Edward McNall Burns (1967).

14. *The Federalist Papers* references will be cited in the text, with the number and page; the referenced edition is the Clinton Rossiter-prepared text (1961).

15. Burns (1967) in chapters 2 and 3 elaborates on these distinctions; also see Krouse (1983).

16. Krouse (1983), p. 65; emphasis in original.

17. James Madison to Thomas Jefferson, 24 October 1787; in Michael Kammen's (1966) collection, p. 73.

18. Krouse (1983), p. 64.

19. Charles W. Anderson (1993), p. 219; also see Burns (1967).

20. Hamilton is quoted in Dahl (1956), p. 7.

21. Two classic references chronicling these times and transformation

are Arthur M. Schlesinger Jr. (1945) and George Dangerfield (1965); also Morone (1990), chapter 2.

22. Richard Heffner in De Tocqueville (1956), p. 10. Direct references of De Tocqueville (1956) will be in the text, by volume and page, in the Heffner edition, unless otherwise noted.

23. DeTocqueville's *Democracy in America* is acknowledged as one of the most compelling texts in American political thought. Still, it is worth noting that some parts are flawed by De Tocqueville's willingness to extrapolate from (what today we would call) inadequate observations. For example, his comments on why Americans have "No Aptitude and No Taste for Science, Literature, or Art" or "Why Americans Are More Addicted to Practical than to Theoretical Science" are sorely hindered by his purview. Similarly, his characterization of a weak president was questionable ("The President . . . possesses almost royal prerogatives, which he has no opportunity of exercising, . . ." 1, p. 80), even at the time, and surely not presently pertinent. Still, that hardly dims the sagacity of many of his observations.

24. Marvin Zetterbaum (1967), p. 54.

25. Krouse (1983), p. 62; emphases in original.

26. Two valuable readings of De Tocqueville are volumes edited with commentary by John Stone and Stephen Mennell (1980) that treats him from a sociologist's perspective, and Zetterbaum (1967).

27. Krouse (1983), p. 69.

28. Dahl (1990), p. 10.

29. As Dryzek and Douglas Torgerson (1993), p. 138 point out, Mill (in 1835) was largely sympathetic to De Tocqueville's need for open discussion and deliberation among citizens. Still, Mill (like Madison) feared the excesses of the unbridled majority and argued for a "right idea of democracy" in which government would be provided by an "enlightened minority" of experts and officials. They conclude: "Despite his significant participatory gestures, Mill's vision of liberal democracy thus paradoxically sought refuge in the expanding administrative apparatus of the modern state."

30. Dewey (1927), p. 146.

31. Krouse (1983), p. 72.

32. Mill (1961), p. xx.

33. Quoted in Carole Pateman (1970), p. 30.

34. Krouse (1983), p. 74.

35. Zetterbaum (1967), p. 103.

36. Dahl (1956), p. 46.

37. Dahl (1990), p. 26; emphases in original.

38. Mark Landy (1993), p. 19.

39. Sandel (1996), p. 6

40. The case is made with particular clarity in Dahl's *After the Revolution* (1990).

41. Dahl (1990), p. 118; his numerical "guestimate" is on p. 54.

42. Samuel Huntington (1981), p. 219, and Daniel P. Moynihan (1969), p. 164.

43. Kathy E. Ferguson (1984), pp. 51–80.

44. Peregrine Schwartz-Shea and Debra Burrington (1990), pp. 2–3.

45. Ibid., pp. 31–32; emphasis in original. I am deeply indebted to Gina Guarascio for having raised my consciousness regarding feminist politics.

46. Morone (1990), p. 1; cf. Dryzek (1989).

47. Morone (1990), p. 7.

48. Ibid., p. 29.

49. Ibid., p. 30.

50. Putnam (1995).

51. Greider (1992), p. 15.

52. Lasch (1995).

53. Also see C. George Benello and Dimitrious Poussopoulous (1971), and Stuart Langton (1978).

54. G. D. H. Cole (1919), *Self-Government in Industry*, p. 157; quoted in Pateman (1970), p. 38.

55. Pateman (1970), pp. 38 and 42; emphases added.

56. Gabriel A. Almond and Sidney Verba (1965), p. 143.

57. Pateman (1970), p. 110.

58. Jane J. Mansbridge (1980), p. 4.

59. Quoted by Mansbridge (1980), p. 20.

60. Greider (1992), p. 18.

61. All four quotations in these two paragraphs from Mansbridge (1990), pp. 23, 35, and 274; emphases added.

62. For a discussion of contingency theories, the best source remains Paul R. Lawrence and Jay W. Lorsch (1969).

63. James S. Coleman (1990), pp. 302, 303; emphasis in original.

64. For a contemporary, more organized view of anarchy, see Linda deLeon (1994).

65. Putnam (1995), figure 5, p. 675; also see figure 6, p. 676.

66. Ibid., (1993), p. 177; emphasis in original. For a multinational comparison of social capital by another name, that is, trust, see Francis Fukuyama (1995).

67. Greider (1992), p. 19.

68. John W. Gardner (1980), in an address to the Cosmos Club, Washington, D.C.

69. Richard L. Berke (1994), pp. A1, A9.

70. See, for instance, the late Lasch's (1995) list.

73. Dahl (1990), p. 119, under one of his principles for governing, the Criterion of Efficiency.

74. All quotations in this paragraph from Dahl's *Democracy and Its Critics* (1989).

75. Both quotations from Putnam (1993), p. 183.

3. Democratic Foundations of the Policy Sciences

1. See Dewey (1927) as well as Judith N. Shklar (1991); in *A Pre-View of Policy Sciences* (1971), pp. xiii–xiv; Lasswell declares that "The policy sciences are a contemporary adaptation of the general approach to public policy that was recommended by John Dewey and his colleages in the development of American pragmatism."

2. Lasswell (1949a).

3. Ronald D. Brunner (1991), p. 71.

4. Lasswell (1951b), p. 14; for an example, see Lasswell's presidential address to the American Political Science Association (1956).

5. Lasswell (1951b), p. 15. In 1965, Lasswell returned to this theme, describing democracy as an integral feature for the "wide sharing of power in the community. . . ." (1965), p. 45.

6. Lasswell and Abraham Kaplan (1950), p. 15; also see Lasswell (1951b) for a similar observation, and (1965), p. 35, "we are concerned with the dignity of man."

7. Mark Warren (1992), Mansbridge (1980), and Sandel (1996).

8. Anderson (1993), p. 217; emphasis in original.

9. Warren (1992), p. 9.

10. Anderson (1993), pp. 217 and 218; emphases in original.

11. Ibid., p. 217.

12. Ibid., p. 219.

13. Ibid., p. 220.

14. Dryzek (1993b), p. 218.

15. Brunner (1991), p. 72; emphasis in original.

16. Edith Stokey and Richard Zeckhauser (1978), p. 151; emphasis added.

17. Milton Friedman (1953), p. 5; emphases added.

18. The distinction in terms of energy policy is made quite clear by Paul C. Stern (1986). The phrase "target population" was popularized by Helen Ingram and Anne Schneider (e.g., 1993).

19. See George W. Downs and Patrick D. Larkey (1985), and Dale Whittington and Duncan MacRae Jr. (1986) for discussions.

20. Lasch (1995), p. 79.

21. Max Weber (1946), pp. 232–233.

22. The technocracy versus democracy argument is well-laid out by Jenkins-Smith (1990). There is not a necessary division between the two; see Richard Sclove (1993).

23. Sidney Verba and his colleagues (1993) find that while political activitists might be representative of the public at large in terms of attitudes, they differ substantially in their demographic attributes, economic needs, and government benefits they receive; these differences naturally reflect themselves in different political priorities.

24. For years I have wanted to write a policy article for a professional journal entitled, "If You Think My Theory Is Weak, Wait Until You See My Data." For a more serious review of the former, see Amitai Etzioni (1988); for the latter, see Mark Maier (1991), and Constance F. Citro and Eric A. Hanushek (1991).

25. Dahl (1990).

26. All quotations from Jason DeParle (1994), p. A10.

27. Ingram and Anne Schneider (1993), p. 88.

28. See William Ascher (1986, 1987) for possible explanations; one explanation is an overreliance on positivism; also P. deLeon (1988).

29. Rivlin (1984), p. 319. Rivlin later reiterated her warning to her economist colleagues during her presidential address to the American Economics Association, "If a golden age of economists' self-confidence ever occurred, it is long since past" (1987), p. 1.

30. Eric Hanushek is quoted by Julie Kosterlitz (1991), p. 2412. See the National Reseach Council report, edited by Citro and Hanushek (1991).

31. Brunner (1991), p. 77.

32. Dryzek (1990), pp. 4–6.

33. Fishkin (1991), p. 57; emphasis in original.

34. Louise G. White (1994), p. 506.

35. Jenkins-Smith (1990), p. 69.

36. Perhaps the most trenchant critic of this position, one who argues consistently for the primacy of lay over expert knowledge is Charles E. Lindblom (1990 and, with David K. Cohen, 1979).

37. Warren (1992), p. 10.

38. Ibid.

39. Most prominently, beginning with Theodore J. Lowi (1969).

40. Warren (1992), p. 9.

41. Sandel (1996).

42. Anderson (1992), p. 221.

43. Ibid.

44. Ingram and Schneider (1993).

45. Quoted by Elizabeth Drew (1994), p. 193; also see Adam Clyner, Robert Pear, and Robin Toner (1994).

46. Both quotations in this paragraph from Warren (1992), pp. 11 and 12.

47. Scolve (1993), and John Bridger Robinson (1992).

48. Henry Kariel (1966), p. 67.

49. Fischer (1993) provides a few brief examples; also see Robert Paehlke (1990), and Dryzek (1993a).

50. Dryzek (1989), p. 98.

51. Jenkins-Smith (1990).

52. Lasswell (1949b), Dryzek (1989), and Jenkins-Smith (1990).

53. See Martin Greenberger et al. (1983); also Barry Commoner (1979).

54. Paul Bracken and Martin Shubik (1982).

55. See Fred Kaplan's *Wizards of Armageddon* (1983).

56. Cf. Jonathan Schell (1982) with Joseph S. Nye Jr. (1986).

57. Fox Butterfield (1982), p. 14; a more complete discussion is found in P. deLeon (1987), chapter 5.

58. Not surprisingly, much of this discussion parallels the discussions comparing policy analysis and ethics; see Douglas Amy (1984).

4. The Policy Sciences for Democracy

1. Fischer (1993b), pp. 33–34.

2. Henry Aaron (1978), p. 18.

3. There are multiple accounts on the shortcomings of the policy sciences; see Ascher (1987), P. deLeon (1988), and Davis B. Bobrow and Dryzek (1987).

4. Lasswell (1951b), p. 14.

5. Torgerson (1992), p. 225.

6. Lawrence H. Tribe (1972), and Lasswell (1971).

7. A splendid example is found in Gary King, Robert O. Keohane, and Sidney Verba (1994), as they make careful comparisons between the two research poles.

8. Abraham Kaplan (1963), p. 92.

9. Bruce L. R. Smith (1992).

10. Ingram and Smith (1993), p. 1. Ingram and Schneider (1993), p. 71 are more direct: "Our central purpose is to identify policies that foster democratic participation."

11. Carol Hirschon Weiss (1991), pp. 327–328; also see Downs and Larkey (1985).

12. Robert Klitgaard (1988).

13. For a thoughtful discussion of principal agents theory in a governmental setting, see Terry M. Moe (1984).

14. P. deLeon (1993).

15. Merton (1968), p. 127.

16. James Scott (1972), and Michael Johnston (1982).

17. Poindexter is quoted in P. deLeon (1993), p. 193.

18. Merton (1968), p. 135.

19. Susan Rose-Ackerman (1978), p. 216.

20. Bernard D. Rostker and Scott Harris (1993).

21. David C. Paris and James F. Reynolds (1983); also see M. E. Hawkesworth (1988).

22. Giandomenico Majone (1989), and Fischer (1985).

23. John W. Kingdon (1984), and David A. Rochefort and Roger W. Cobb (1994).

24. Paul A. Sabatier and Jenkins-Smith (1993), and Frank R. Baumgartner and Bryan D. Jones (1993).

25. Yehezkel Dror (1983). Similarly, Wildavsky (1979) divided policy research into "intellectual cognition" and "social interaction."

26. Martin Rein (1976), p. 13. Also see Rein (1983). Rein has drawn upon the seminal work of Karl Mannheim (1936).

27. See Rein and Donald Schön (1993), and Schön and Rein (1994).

28. Stone (1988); also see Thomas J. Kaplan (1993).

29. Rein (1976), p. 85.

30. Rein and Schön (1993), p. 159.

31. Maarten A. Hajer (1993), pp. 45 and 47.

32. Torgerson (1986), p. 34.

33. Much of this is laid out by Richard J. Bernstein (1983).

34. Fischer (1990), and Laurence E. Lynn Jr. (1994, 1996) provide backgrounds in the development of scientific management, although they reach differing conclusions. "Clinical reason" was coined by Stone (1993); quotation from p. 65.

35. Weiss (1991), p. 320.

36. Torgerson (1986), footnote 4, pp. 52–53; emphases in original.

37. See, for instance, Graham Burchell, Colin Gordon, and Peter Miller (1991), for a general introduction to Foucault as well as to some of his essays; also Michel Foucault (1980). Hermeneutics is described by Roberto Alejandro (1993) and Paul Diesing (1991). The interpretivist literature is represented by, among others, M. E. Hawkesworth (1988) and Dvora Yanow (1995a, 1995b). Again, it is important to note that these frames are treated here independently for purposes of explication, although there are key commonalities.

38. Torgerson (1993), p. 16.

39. Foucault's "Governmentability" is printed in Burchell, Colin Gordon, and Miller (1991), chapter 4.

40. Both quotations from Marie Danziger (1995), pp. 435 and 441.

41. Torgerson (1993), p. 18.

42. Dryzek (1982), p. 322; also see Diesing (1991).

43. Both quotations from Alejandro (1993), p. 36.

44. Both quotations from Yanow (1995b and 1995a), pp. 117, 118 (emphases added), and 419, respectively. In this latter essay, Professor Yanow proposes a physical space—a literal building—as part of an interpretative policy analysis.

45. Torgerson (1986), p. 40; emphasis in original.

46. See Rolf Wiggershaus (1994) for a careful review of the Frankfurt School. Included in its alumni are Herbert Marcuse, Erich Fromm, Theodore Adorno, and Max Horkheimer.

47. There is, of course, extensive literature on Jürgen Habermas, both by his own pen (see Habermas [1979, 1983, and 1987] for instance) and those of others (e.g., Fischer and Forester [1987]; Forester [1985 and 1993]; Richard Bernstein [1985]; and Jane Braaten, [1991]). Also see Dryzek (1990) and Bobrow and Dryzek (1987), chapter 11, who drew heavily from Habermas to formulate "critical policy analysis."

48. Daniel Yankelovich (1991), p. 212.

49. Jane Braaten (1991), p. 11.

50. John Forester (1993), p. 39; Dryzek (1990), chapter 1, is even more critical of the capabilities of instrumental rationality in terms of policy research.

51. Both quotations from Braaten (1991), pp. 7 and 13.

52. Yankelovich (1991), p. 213.

53. Braaten (1991), p. 89.

54. Bobrow and Dryzek (1987), pp. 169, 170.

55. Roy Kemp (1985), p. 188.

56. Dryzek (1990), p. 43.

57. Yankelovich (1991), pp. 216, 217.

58. Warren (1992), p. 12.

59. Kemp (1985), and Frank N. Laird (1990).

60. Kemp (1985), pp. 177 and 197–98; emphases added.

61. Stanford F. Schram (1995); see Forester's acerbic rebuttal (1995).

62. Dryzek (1982, 1989, and 1990), and Torgerson (1986). The source documents for the two Berger commissions are Berger (1977 and 1985).

63. Berger (1977), p. 228.

64. Bobrow and Dryzek (1987), p. 172.

65. Forester (1985), p. 261.

66. Both quotations from Forester (1993), pp. 72 and 145.

67. Amitai Etzioni (1988).

68. Rein (1976 and 1983) and Douglas Amy (1984).

69. Both quotations from Dryzek (1990), p. 72.

70. Ingram and Smith (1993).

71. Robert B. Denhardt (1981), p. 633.

72. Fischer (1993a), p. 183.

5. The Policy Sciences of Democracy: ... Two Roads Diverged

1. William Barrett (1979).

2. Denhardt (1981), pp. 631, 633.

3. Dryzek (1990).

4. Dan Durning (1993), Fischer (1992), and P. deLeon (1992).

5. Kolakowski is quoted by Torgerson (1992), p. 225.

6. Schwartz (1988), p. 8.

7. Robert E. Goodin (1993), pp. 237–238 and 240; this view compares favorably with Anderson's view of "liberal rationalism" (1993).

8. Lippmann's positions are described by Lasch (1995).

9. Dewey (1927), pp. 208–209, 211, 218; emphasis in original.

10. Verba (1996), p. 4.

11. Dionne (1991), Greider (1992), Sandel (1996), and Lasch (1995).

12. Yankelovich (1994), p. 51.

13. Dewey (1927), p. 34.

14. See Fishkin (1991); emphasis in original.

15. As reported in the Poll Watch for 13 February 1996, published by the Pew Research Center for the People & the Press (formerly the Times-Mirror Center for the People & the Press), p. 3.

16. Robert B. Denhardt (1981), p. 632.

17. Ibid., both quotations from p. 633.

18. Michael Barzelay (1992).

19. Forester (1993), p. 58.

20. Lasswell (1951a) is recalled by Torgerson (1986), p. 42; emphasis in original.

21. Brunner and William Ascher (1992), p. 324; Richard Rose (1989), p. 6; and Lindblom (1986), p. 361. Cf. Rose (1989) with Ingram and Schneider (1993); also Brunner and Ascher (1992) with Howard Margolis (1996).

22. Sandel (1996), p. 321.

23. Bobrow and Dryzek (1987), p. 176.

24. Forester (1993), p. 151.

25. Daniel Goleman (1992) p. B–5.

26. Melvin M. Webber (1978), pp. 158 and 159.

27. Patsy Healy (1993), p. 241.

28. John Friedmann (1973), chapter 7; both quotations from p. 190; emphases in orginal.

29. Forester (1988), p. 21; emphases in original.

30. See Colleen Cordes (1996a); also Cordes (1996b), and Bruce L. R. Smith (1992). Important work on nonprofit organizations and their willingness to involve citizens has been published by Verba, Kay Lehman Schlozman, and Henry E. Brady (1995).

31. Denhardt (1981), p. 633.

32. Durning (1993), p. 300.

33. This proposal is sympathetic to, but distinct from, the participatory methodology reported by Marisa Kelly and Steven Maynard-Moody (1993), in that the latter employs evaluation sessions using exclusively stakeholders.

34. Ortwin Renn et al. (1993), pp. 191 and 206.

35. Fishkin (1991), p. 9; cf. this with Dewey, endnote 9, and Renn et al. (1993).

36. Dahl (1989), p. 340.

37. Ned Crosby, Janet Keller, and Paul Shaefer (1986). Dahl (1992), p. 55, and Fishkin (1991), pp. 96–97.

38. Lyn Kathlene and John A. Martin (1991), p. 61.

39. The survey is described by Michael Kinsley (1996), p. 4.

40. Kathlene and Martin (1991), pp. 47–48.

41. Jenkins-Smith (1990), p. 199.

42. Renn et al. (1993), p. 210.

43. Robinson (1992), pp. 249 and 251; also see Margolis (1996).

44. See Steven Kelman (1989), for instance.

45. See Jane Braxton Little (1996), p. 4. Examples of "connected" include allowing members of the homeless community in Maine to use a park as a voting registration address. On a much larger survey, see Almond and Verba's (1965) comparison of five nations and their rates of participation.

46. Sabatier and Anne Brasher (1993).

47. Fischer (1993a).

48. Renn et al. (1993), p. 191.

49. Ibid., p. 209.

50. Jeffrey M. Berry, Kent E. Portnoy, and Ken Thomson (1993), p. 212.

51. Ibid., pp. 254–255.

52. William E. Lyons, David Lowry, and Ruth Hoogland deHoog (1992). As an aside, their findings deal a serious blow to the public choice theory that celebrates the putative benefits resulting from decentralization.

53. See the postpositivist examination of social welfare policy by Stanford F. Schram (1993) as an example.

54. Warren (1996), p. 47.

55. Danzinger (1995).

56. See the essays collected by Ingram and Smith (1993) on designing policies to encourage democratic procedures.

57. See Rivlin (1992a, 1992b) for examples.

58. Denhardt (1981).

59. Jane Aronson (1993), p. 375.

60. David L. Kirp (1992).

61. Both quotations from Edward F. Lawlor (1996), p. 120.

62. Berry, Portney, and Thomson (1993), p. 293.

63. John Robinson (1982).

BIBLIOGRAPHY

Aaron, Henry. 1978. *Politics and the Professors: The Great Society in Perspective.* Washington, DC: Brookings Institution.

Alejandro, Roberto. 1993. *Hermeneutics, Citizenship, and the Public Sphere.* Albany: State University of New York Press.

Almond, Gabriel A., and Sidney Verba. 1965. *The Civic Culture.* Boston: Little, Brown.

Amy, Douglas. 1984. "Why Policy Analysis and Ethics Are Incompatible." *Journal of Policy Analysis and Management.* Vol. 3, No. 4 (Summer). Pp. 573–591.

Anderson, Charles W. 1993. "Recommending a Scheme of Reason: Political Theory, Policy Science, and Democracy." *Policy Sciences.* Vol. 26, No. 3. Pp. 367–378.

Aronson, Jane. 1993. "Giving Consumers a Say in Policy Development: Influencing Policy or Just Being Heard?" *Canadian Public Policy.* Vol. 19, No. 4. Pp. 367–378.

Ascher, William. 1986. "The Evolution of the Policy Sciences." *Journal of Policy Analysis and Management.* Vol. 5, No. 2 (Winter). Pp. 365–389.

———. 1987. "Policy Sciences and the Economic Approach in a 'Post-Positivist' World." *Policy Sciences.* Vol. 20, No. 1 (April). Pp. 3–9.

Barber, Benjamin. 1984. *Strong Democracy: Participatory Politics for a New Age.* Berkeley: University of California Press.

Barrett, William. 1979. *The Illusion of Technique.* Garden City, NY: Anchor/Doubleday.

Barzelay, Michael. 1992. *Breaking Through Bureaucracy.* Berkeley: University of California Press.

143

Baumgartner, Frank R., and Bryan D. Jones. 1993. *Agendas and Instability in American Politics*. Chicago: University of Chicago Press.

Benello, C. George, and Dimitrious Poussopolous (Eds.). 1971. *The Case for Participatory Democracy*. New York: Grossman.

Berger, Thomas R. 1977. *Northern Frontier, Northern Homeland: Report of the MacKenzie Valley Pipeline Commission*. Toronto: James Lorimer.

———. 1985. *Village Journey: The Report of the Alaskan Native Review Commission*. New York: Hill & Wang.

Berke, Richard L. 1994. "Anger and Cynicism Well Up In Voters as Hope Gives Way." *New York Times*. 10 October. Pp. A1, A9.

Bernstein, Richard J. 1983. *Beyond Objectivism and Relativism*. Philadelphia: University of Pennsylvania Press.

——— (Ed.). 1985. *Habermas and Modernity*. Cambridge, MA: MIT Press.

Berry, Jeffrey M., Kent E. Portney, and Ken Thomson. 1993. *The Rebirth of Urban Democracy*. Washington, DC: Brookings Institution.

Braaten, Jane. 1991. *Habermas's Critical Theory of Society*. Albany: State University of New York Press.

Bracken, Paul, and Martin Shubik. 1982. "Strategic War: What Are the Questions and Who Should Be Asking Them?" *Technology in Society*. Vol. 4, No. 2. Pp. 155–179.

Bobrow, Davis B., and John S. Dryzek. 1987. *Policy Analysis by Design*. Pittsburgh, PA: University of Pittsburgh Press.

Brunner, Ronald D. 1991. "The Policy Movement as a Policy Problem." *Policy Sciences*. Vol. 24, No. 1 (February). Pp. 65–98.

———, and William Ascher. 1992. "Science and Social Responsibility." *Policy Sciences*. Vol. 25, No. 3 (August). Pp. 295–331.

Burchell, Graham, Colin Gordon, and Peter Miller (Eds.). 1991. *The Foucault Effect: Studies in Governmentality*. Chicago: University of Chicago Press.

Burns, Edward McNall. 1967. *James Madison: Philosopher of the Constitution*. New York: Farrar.

Butterfield, Fox. 1982. "Anatomy of the Nuclear Protest." *New York Times Magazine*. 11 July. Pp. 12–16, 48–49.

Citro, Constance F., and Eric A. Hanushek (Eds.). 1991. *Improving Information for Social Policy Decisions: The Uses of Microsimulation Modeling*. Washington, DC: National Academy Press.

Clymer, Adam, Robert Pear, and Robin Toner. 1994. "For Health Care, Time Was a Killer." *New York Times*. 29 August. Pp. A1, A8, A9.

Cohen, Carl. 1971. *Democracy*. Athens: University of Georgia Press.

Cohen, Joshua, and Joel Rogers. 1981. *On Democracy*. New York: Penguin Books.

Coleman, James S. 1990. *Foundations of Social Theory*. Cambridge, MA: Belknap for Harvard University Press.

Commoner, Barry. 1979. *The Politics of Energy*. New York: Knopf.

Cordes, Colleen. 1996a. "NIH Says that Makeup of Advisory Panels Can Influence Findings." *Chronicle of Higher Education*. Vol. 42, No. 26 (8 March). P. A27.

———. 1996b. "Critics Say Membership of Federal Science Panels Is Too Narrow." *Chronicle of Higher Education*. Vol. 42, No. 26 (8 March). P. A26.

Crosby, Ned, Janet Kelley, and Paul Shaefer (1986). "Citizens Panels: A New Approach to Citizen Participation." *Public Administration Review*. Vol. 46, No. 2 (March/April). Pp. 170–179.

Dahl, Robert A. 1956. *A Preface to Democratic Theory*. Chicago: University of Chicago Press.

———. 1989. *Democracy and Its Critics*. New Haven, CT: Yale University Press.

———. 1990. *After the Revolution*. New Haven: Yale University Press. Originally published in 1970.

———. 1992. "The Problem of Civil Competence." *Journal of Democracy*. Vol. 3, No. 4 (October). Pp. 45–59.

Dangerfield, George. 1965. *The Awakening of American Nationalism*. New York: Harper.

Danziger, Marie. 1995. "Policy Analysis Postmodernized." *Policy Studies Journal*. Vol. 23, No. 3 (Fall). Pp. 435–450.

deLeon, Linda. 1994. "Embracing Anarchy: Network Organizations and Interorganizational Networks." *Administrative Theory & Praxis*. Vol. 16, No. 2. Pp. 234–253.

deLeon, Peter. 1987. *The Altered Strategic Environment: Towards the Year 2000*. Lexington, MA: Lexington Books.

———. 1988. *Advice and Consent: The Development of Policy Sciences*. New York: Russell Sage Foundation.

————. 1992. "The Democratization of the Policy Sciences." *Public Adminis-tration Review*. Vol. 52, No. 2 (March/April). Pp. 125–129.

————. 1993. *Thinking about Political Corruption*. Armonk, NY: M. E. Sharpe.

Denhardt, Robert B. 1981. "Towards a Critical Theory of Public Organiza-tion." *Public Administration Review*. Vol. 41, No. 6 (November/De-cember). Pp. 628–635.

DeParle, Jason. 1994. "The Clinton Welfare Bill Begins Trek in Congress." *New York Times*. 15 July. Pp. A1, A10.

De Tocqueville, Alexis. 1956. *Democracy in America* (Ed.). Richard D. Heff-ner. New York: Mentor. Two Volumes, originally published in English in 1835 and 1840.

————. 1980. *[Selected Writings] On Democracy, Revolution, and Society* (Eds.). John Stone and Stephen Mennell. Chicago: University of Chicago Press.

Dewey, John. 1927. *The Public and Its Problems*. Denver: Alan Swallow.

Diesing, Paul. 1991. *How Does Social Science Work?* Pittsburgh: University of Pittsburgh Press.

Dionne, E. J. 1991. *Why Americans Hate Politics*. New York: Simon & Schuster.

Downs, George W., and Patrick D. Larkey. 1985. *The Search for Governmen-tal Efficiency*. Philadelphia: Temple University Press.

Drew, Elizabeth. 1994. *On the Edge: The Clinton Presidency*. New York: Si-mon & Schuster.

Dror, Yehezkel. 1983. "Policy-Gambling: A Preliminary Exploration." *Policy Studies Journal*. Vol. 12, No. 1 (September). Pp. 6–16.

Dryzek, John S. 1982. "Policy Analysis as a Hermeneutic Activity." *Policy Sciences*. Vol. 14, No. 4 (August). Pp. 309–331.

————. 1989. "Policy Sciences of Democracy." *Polity*. Vol. 22, No. 1 (Fall). Pp. 97–118.

————. 1990. *Discursive Democracy*. New York: Cambridge University Press.

————. 1993a. "Informal Logic in the Design of Politics and Institutions." Paper presented to the Annual Meeting of the American Political Sci-ence Association, Washington, DC.

————. 1993b. "Policy Analysis and Planning: From Science to Argument." In Frank Fischer and John Forester (Eds.). 1993. *The Argumentative*

Turn in Policy Analysis and Planning. Durham, NC: Duke University Press.

———, and Douglas Torgerson. 1993. "Democracy and the Policy Sciences." *Policy Sciences*. Vol. 26, No. 3 (Autumn). Pp. 127–138.

Duncan, Graeme (Ed.). 1983. *Democratic Theory and Practice*. New York: Oxford University Press.

Durning, Dan. 1993. "Participatory Policy Analysis in a Social Service Agency: A Case Study." *Journal of Policy Analysis and Management*. Vol. 12, No. 2 (Spring). Pp. 231–257.

Etzioni, Amitai. 1988. *The Moral Dimension*. New York: Free Press.

Ferguson, Kathy E. 1984. *The Feminist Case Against Bureaucracy*. Philadelphia: Temple University Press.

Fischer, Frank. 1985. "Critical Evaluation of Public Policy: A Methodological Case Study." In John Forester (Ed.). 1985. *Critical Theory and Public Life*. Cambridge, MA: MIT Press.

———. 1990. *Technocracy and the Politics of Expertise*. Newbury Park, CA: Sage Publications.

———. 1992. "Restructuring Policy Analysis: A Postpositivist Perspective." *Policy Sciences*. Vol. 25, No. 3 (August). Pp. 333–339.

———. 1993a. "Citizen Participation and the Democratization of Policy Expertise." *Policy Sciences*. Vol. 26, No. 3 (August). Pp. 165–188.

———. 1993b. "Policy Discourse and the Politics of Washington Think Tanks." In Frank Fischer and John Forester (Eds.). 1993. *The Argumentative Turn in Policy Analysis and Planning*. Durham, NC: Duke University Press.

———, and John Forester (Eds.). 1987. *Confronting Values in Policy Analysis*. Newbury Park, CA: Sage Publications.

Fishkin, James S. 1991. *Democracy and Deliberation*. New Haven, CT: Yale University Press.

Forester, John. 1985. "The Policy Analysis-Critical Theory Affair: Wildavsky and Habermas as Bedfellows?" In John Forester (Ed.). 1985. *Critical Theory and Public Life*. Cambridge, MA: MIT Press.

———. 1988. *Planning in the Face of Power*. Berkeley: University of California Press.

———. 1993. *Critical Theory, Public Policy, and Planning Practice*. Albany: State University of New York Press.

———. 1995. "Response: Toward a Critical Theory of Sociology." *Policy Sciences*. Vol. 28, No. 4 (November). Pp. 385–396.

Foucault, Michel. 1980. *Power/Knowledge.* New York: Pantheon.

Friedman, Milton. 1953. *Essays in Positive Economics.* Chicago: University of Chicago Press.

Friedmann, John. 1973. *Retracking America: A Theory of Transactive Planning.* Garden City, NY: Doubleday/Anchor.

Fukuyama, Francis. 1995. *Trust: The Social Virtues and the Creation of Prosperity.* New York: Free Press.

Galbraith, John Kenneth. 1996. *The Good Society: The Human Agenda.* Boston: Houghton.

Gardner, John W. 1980. "The War of the Parts Against the Whole." Washington, DC: Speech before the Cosmos Club, 3 April.

Goldhamer, Herbert. 1978. *The Adviser.* New York: American Elsevier.

Goleman, Daniel. 1992. "Architects Rediscover the Best City Planners: Citizens." *New York Times.* 2 June. Pp. B–5, B–9.

Goodin, Robert E. 1993. "Democracy, Preferences and Paternalism." *Policy Sciences.* Vol. 26, No. 3. Pp. 229–248.

Greenberger, Martin, et al. 1983. *Caught Unawares.* Cambridge, MA: Ballinger.

Greider, William. 1992. *Who Will Tell the People: The Betrayal of American Democracy.* New York: Simon & Schuster (Touchstone).

Guinier, Lani. 1994. *The Tyranny of the Majority.* New York: Free Press.

Habermas, Jürgen. 1979. *Communication and the Evolution of Society.* Thomas McCarthy (Trans.). Boston: Beacon.

———. 1983. *The Theory of Communicative Action: Reason and the Rationalization of Society.* Thomas McCarthy (Trans.). Vol. 1. Boston: Beacon.

———. 1987. *The Theory of Communicative Action: Lifeworld and System: A Critique of Functionalist Reason.* Vol. 2. Thomas McCarthy (Trans.). Boston: Beacon.

Hajer, Maarten A. 1993. "Discourse Coalitions and the Institutionalization of Practice." In Frank Fischer and John Forester (Eds.). 1993. *The Argumentative Turn in Policy Analysis and Planning.* Durham, NC: Duke University Press.

Hamilton, Alexander, James Madison, and John Jay. 1961. *The Federalist Papers.* Introduction by Clinton Rossiter. New York: New American Library. Originally published in the "McLean Edition" of 1788.

Hawkesworth, M. E. 1988. *Theoretical Issues of Policy Analysis.* Albany: State University of New York Press.

Healy, Patsy. 1993. "Planning Through Debate: The Communicative Turn in Planning Theory." In Frank Fischer and John Forester (Eds.). 1993. *The Argumentative Turn in Policy Analysis and Planning.* Durham, NC: Duke University Press.

Horowitz, Irving Louis. 1981. "Social Science and the Reagan Administration." *Journal of Policy Analysis and Management.* Vol. 1, No. 1 (Fall). Pp. 126–129.

Huntington, Samuel. 1981. *American Politics: The Promise of Disharmony.* Cambridge, MA: Harvard University Press.

Ingram, Helen, and Anne Schneider. 1991. "The Choice of Target Populations." *Administration & Society.* Vol. 23, No. 3 (November). Pp. 333–356.

———. 1993. "Constructing Citizenship: The Subtle Messages of Policy Design." In Helen Ingram and Steven Ragthed Smith (Eds.). 1993. *Public Policies for Democracy.* Washington, DC: Brookings Institution.

Ingram, Helen, and Steven Ragthed Smith (Eds.). 1993. *Public Policies for Democracy.* Washington, DC: Brookings Institution.

Jenkins-Smith, Hank C. 1990. *Democratic Politics and Policy Analysis.* Pacific Grove, CA: Brooks/Cole.

Johnston, Michael. 1982. *Political Corruption and Public Policy in America.* Monterey, CA: Cole Publishing.

Kammen, Michael (Ed.). 1966. *The Origins of the American Constitution: Private Correspondence of the Founders.* New York: Penguin.

Kaplan, Abraham. 1963. *American Ethics and Public Policy.* New York: Oxford University Press.

Kaplan, Fred. 1983. *The Wizards of Armageddon.* New York. Simon & Schuster.

Kaplan, Thomas J. 1993. "Reading Policy Narratives: Beginnings, Middles, and Ends. In Frank Fischer and John Forester (Eds.). 1993. *The Argumentative Turn in Policy Analysis and Planning.* Durham, NC: Duke University Press.

Kariel, Henry. 1966. *The Promise of Politics.* Englewood Cliffs, NJ: Prentice-Hall.

Kathlene, Lyn, and John A. Martin. 1991. "Enhancing Citizen Participation: Panel Designs, Perspectives, and Policy Formation." *Journal of Policy Analysis and Management.* Vol. 10, No. 1 (Winter). Pp. 46–63.

Kelley, Marisa, and Steven Maynard-Moody (1993). "Policy Analysis in the Post-Positivist Era: Engaging Stakeholders in Evaluating the Economic Development District Programs." *Public Administration Review*. Vol. 53, No. 2 (March/April). Pp. 135–142.

Kelman, Steven. 1987. *Making Public Policy*. New York. Basic.

Kemp, Roy. 1985. "Planning, Public Hearings, and the Politics of Discourse." In John Forester (Ed.). 1985. *Critical Theory and Public Life*. Cambridge, MA. MIT Press.

King, Gary, Robert O. Keohane, and Sidney Verba. 1994. *Designing Social Inquiry: Scientific Inference in Qualitative Research*. Cambridge, MA: Harvard University Press.

Kingdon, John W. 1984. *Agendas, Alternatives, and Public Policies*. Boston: Little, Brown.

Kinsley, Michael. 1996. "The Intellectual Free Lunch." *The New Yorker*. Vol. 71, No. 45 (19 February). Pp. 4–5.

Kirp, David L. 1992. "The End of Policy Analysis: With Apologies to Daniel (*End of Ideology*) Bell and Francis ("The End of History") Fukuyama." *Journal of Policy Analysis and Management*. Vol. 11, No. 4 (Fall). Pp. 693–696.

Klitgaard, Robert. 1988. *Controlling Corruption*. Berkeley: University of California Press.

Kosterlitz, Julie. 1991. "Educated Guesswork." *National Journal*. Vol. 23, No. 40 (5 October). Pp. 2408–2413.

Krouse, Richard W. 1983. "'Classical' Images of Democracy in America: Madison and De Tocqueville." In Graeme Duncan (Ed.). 1983. *Democratic Theory and Practice*. Cambridge: Cambridge University Press.

Laird, Frank N. 1990. "Technocracy Revisited: Knowledge, Power, and the Crisis in Energy Decision Making." *Industrial Crisis Quarterly*. Vol. 4, No. 1. Pp. 49–61.

Landy, Mark. 1993. "Public Policy and Citizenship." In Helen Ingram and Stephen Rathgeb Smith (Eds.). 1993. *Public Policies for Democracy*. Washington, DC: Brookings Institution.

Langton, Stuart. (Ed.). 1978. *Citizen Participation in America*. Lexington, MA: Lexington Books.

Lasch, Christopher. 1995. *The Revolt of the Elites and the Betrayal of Democracy*. New York: Norton.

Lasswell, Harold D. 1949a. *Power and Personality*. New York: Norton.

———. 1949b. "The Democratic Character." In his *Political Writings of Harold D. Lasswell*. Glencoe, IL. Pp. 465–525.

———. 1951. "The Policy Orientation." *The Policy Sciences*. In Daniel Lerner and Harold D. Lasswell (Eds.). 1951. Palo Alto, CA: Stanford University Press. Pp. 3–15.

———. 1956. "The Political Science of Science." *American Political Science Review*. Vol. 50, No. 4 (December). Pp. 961–979.

———. 1965. "The World Revolution of Our Time: A Framework for Basic Policy Research." In *World Revolutionary Elites: Studies in Coercive Ideological Movements*. Daniel Lerner and Harold D. Lasswell (Eds.). 1965. Cambridge: MIT Press. Chap. 2.

———. 1971. *A Pre-View of Policy Sciences*. New York: American Elsevier.

———, and Abraham Kaplan. 1950. *Power and Society*. New Haven, CT: Yale University Press.

Lawlor, Edward F. 1996. "Book Reviews." *Journal of Policy Analysis and Management*. Vol. 15, No. 1 (Winter). Pp. 110–121.

Lawrence, Paul R., and Jay W. Lorsch. 1969. *Organizations and Environment*. Homewood, IL: Richard D. Irwin.

Lerner, Daniel, and Harold D. Lasswell (Eds.). 1951. *The Policy Sciences*. Palo Alto, CA: Stanford University Press.

Lindblom, Charles E. (1986). "Who Needs What Social Research or Policymaking?" *Knowledge: Creation, Diffusion, Utilization*. Vol. 7 (June). Pp. 345–366.

———. 1990. *Inquiry and Change*. New Haven, CT: Yale University Press.

———, and David K. Cohen. 1979. *Usable Knowledge*. New Haven, CT: Yale University Press.

Little, Jane Braxton. 1966. "Where People Feel Connected, Voter Turnout Soars." *PA Times*. Vol. 19, No. 2 (1 February). Pp. 4–5.

Lowi, Theodore J. 1969. *The End of Liberalism: Ideology, Policy, and the Crisis of Public Authority*. New York: Norton.

Lynd, Robert S. 1939. *Knowledge for What? The Place of Social Sciences in the American Culture*. Princeton, NJ: Princeton University Press.

Lynn, Jr., Laurence E. (1994). "Public Management Research: The Triumph of Art Over Science." *Journal of Policy Analysis and Management*. Vol. 13, No. 2 (Spring). Pp. 231–259.

———. 1996. *Public Management as Art, Science, and Profession*. Chatham, NJ: Chatham House.

Lyons, William E., David Lowry, and Ruth Hoogland deHoog. 1992. *The Politics of Dissatisfaction*. Armonk, NY: M. E. Sharpe.

Majone, Giandomenico 1989. *Evidence, Argument, & Persuasion in the Policy Process.* New Haven, CT: Yale University Press.

Mannheim, Karl. 1936. *Ideology and Utopia.* Louis Wirth and Edward Shills (Trans.). New York: Harcourt.

Mansbridge, Jane J. 1980. *Beyond Adversary Democracy.* New York: Basic.

Margolis, Howard. 1996. *Dealing with Risk.* Chicago: University of Chicago Press.

Mayo, H. B. 1960. *An Introduction to Democratic Theory.* New York: Oxford University Press.

Maier, Mark H. 1991. *The Data Game.* Armonk, NY: M. E. Sharpe.

Meltsner, Arnold. 1990. *Rules for Rulers: The Politics of Advice.* Philadelphia: Temple University Press.

Merton, Robert K. 1936. "The Unanticipated Consequences of Purposive Social Action." *American Sociological Review.* Vol. 1, No. 4 (December). Pp. 894–904.

———. 1968. *Social Theory and Social Structure.* New York: Free Press. Originally published in 1949.

Mill, John Stuart. 1961. "Introduction." In Alexis De Tocqueville. *Democracy in America* (Trans.). Henry Reeve. New York: Schocken. Originally published in 1835.

Moe, Terry M. 1984. "The New Economics of Organization." *American Journal of Political Science.* Vol. 28, No. 4, (November). Pp. 739–777.

Morone, James A. 1990. *The Democratic Wish.* New York: Basic.

Moynihan, Daniel P. 1969. *Maximum Feasible Misunderstanding: Community Action in the War on Poverty.* New York: Free Press.

Nye, Joseph S. Jr. 1986. *Nuclear Ethics.* New York: Free Press.

Paehlke, Robert. 1990. "Democracy and Environmentalism: Opening a Door to the Administrative State." In Robert Paehlke and Douglas Torgerson (Eds.). 1990. *Managing Leviathan: Environmental Politics and the Administrative State.* Peterborough, Ontario, Canada: Broadview Press.

Paris, David C., and James F. Reynolds. 1983. *The Logic of Policy Inquiry.* New York: Longman.

Pateman, Carole. (1970). *Participation and Democratic Theory.* New York: Cambridge University Press.

Phillips, Kevin. 1994. *Arrogant Capitol: Washington, Wall Street, and the Frustration of American Democracy.* Boston: Little, Brown.

Putnam, Robert D. 1993. *Making Democracy Work: Civic Traditions in Modern Italy*. Princeton, NJ: Princeton University Press.

————. 1994. "Bowling Alone: Democracy in America at the End of the Twentieth Century." Nobel Symposium in Uppsala, Sweden. (August)

————. 1995. "Tuning In, Tuning Out: The Strange Disappearance of Social Capital in the United States." *PS: Political Science and Politics*. Vol. 28, No. 4. Pp. 664–683.

Rein, Martin. 1976. *Social Science and Public Policy*. New York: Penguin.

————. 1983. *From Policy to Practice*. Armonk, NY: M. E. Sharpe.

————, and Donald A. Schön. 1993. "Reframing Policy Discourse." In Frank Fischer and John Forester (Eds.). 1993. *The Argumentative Turn in Policy Analysis and Planning*. Durham, NC: Duke University Press.

Renn, Ortwin, Thomas Webber, Horst Rakel, Peter Dienel, and Brenda Johnson. 1993. "Public Participation in Decision Making: A Three-Step Procedure." *Policy Sciences*. Vol. 26, No. 3 (August). Pp. 189–214.

Rivlin, Alice M. 1984. "A Public Policy Paradox." *Journal of Policy Analysis and Management*. Vol. 4, No. 1 (Fall). Pp. 17–22.

————. 1987. "Economics and the Political Process." *American Economics Review*. Vol. 77, No. 1 (March). Pp. 1–10.

————. 1992a. "A New Vision of American Federalism." *Public Administration Review*. Vol. 52, No. 4 (July/August). Pp. 315–320.

————. 1992b. *Reviving the American Dream*. Washington, DC: Brookings Institution.

Robinson, John Bridger. 1982. "Apples and Horned Toads: On the Framework-Determined Nature of the Energy Debate." *Policy Sciences*. Vol. 15, No. 1 (November). Pp. 23–45.

————. 1992. "Risks, Predictions and Other Optical Illusions: Rethinking the Use of Science in Social Decision-Making." *Policy Sciences*. Vol. 25, No. 3 (August). Pp. 237–255.

Rochefort, David A., and Roger W. Cobb (Eds.). 1994. *The Politics of Problem Definition*. Lawrence: University of Kansas Press.

Rose, Richard. 1989. *Ordinary People in Public Policy*. Newbury Park, CA. Sage Publications.

Rose-Ackerman, Susan. 1978. *Corruption: A Study in Political Economy*. New York: Academic Press.

Rostker, Bernard D., and Scott Harris. (Study Directors). 1993. *Sexual Orientation and U.S. Military Personnel Policy*. Santa Monica, CA: RAND Report MR-3230-OSD.

Sabatier, Paul A., and Anne M. Brasher. 1993. "From Vague Consensus to Clearly Differentiated Coalitions: Environmental Policy at Lake Tahoe." In Paul A. Sabatier and Hank C. Jenkins-Smith (Eds.). 1993. *Policy Change and Learning: An Advocacy Coalition Framework.* Boulder, CO: Westview Press.

Sabatier, Paul A., and Hank C. Jenkins-Smith (Eds.). 1993. *Policy Change and Learning: An Advocacy Coalition Approach.* Boulder, CO: Westview Press.

Sandel, Michael J. 1996. *Democracy's Discontent: America in Search of a Public Philosophy.* Cambridge, MA: Harvard University Press.

Sartori, Giovanni. 1987. *The Theory of Democracy Revisited.* Chatham, NJ: Chatham House.

Schell, Jonathan. 1982. *The Fate of the Earth.* New York: Alfred A. Knopf.

Schlesinger, Arthur M. Jr. 1945. *The Age of Jackson.* Boston: Little, Brown.

Schön, Donald A., and Martin Rein. 1994. *Frame Reflection.* New York: Basic.

Schmitter, Philippe C., and Terry Lynn Karl. 1991. "What Democracy Is . . . and Is Not." *Journal of Democracy.* Vol. 2, No. 3 (Summer). Pp. 75–88.

Schram, Sanford F. 1993. "Postmodern Policy Analysis: Discourse and Identity in Welfare Policy." 1995. *Policy Sciences.* Vol. 26, No. 3 (August). Pp. 249–270.

———. 1995. "Against Policy Analysis: Critical Reason and Poststructural Resistance." *Policy Sciences.* Vol. 28, No. 4 (November). Pp. 375–384.

Schwartz, Nancy L. 1988. *The Blue Guitar: Political Representation and Community.* Chicago: University of Chicago Press.

Schwartz-Shea, Peregrine, and Debra Burrington. 1990. "Free-Riding, Alternative Organization, and Cultural Feminism: The Case of Seneca Women's Peace Camp." *Women in Politics*, Vol. 10, No. 3. Pp. 1–37.

Sclove, Richard. 1993. "Technology Politics As If Democracy Really Mattered: Choices Confronting Progressives." In Michael Shuman and Julie Sweig (Eds.). 1993. *Technology for the Common Good.* Washington, DC: Institute for Policy Studies.

Scott, James. 1972. *Comparative Political Corruption.* Englewood Cliffs, NJ: Prentice-Hall.

Shklar, Judith N. 1991. "Redeeming American Political Thought." *American Political Science Review.* Vol. 85, No. 1 (September). Pp. 3–16.

Smith, Bruce L. R. 1992. *The Advisers.* Washington, DC: Brookings Institution.

Smith, Rogers M. 1993. "Beyond Tocqueville, Myrdal, and Harz: The Multiple Traditions in America." *American Political Science Review.*
Vol. 87, No. 3 (September). Pp. 549–566.

Stern, Paul C. 1986. "What Economics Doesn't Say About Energy Use."
Journal of Policy Analysis and Management. Vol. 5, No. 2 (Winter).
Pp. 200–227.

Stockman, David. 1985. *The Triumph of Politics.* New York: Harper.

Stokey, Edith, and Richard Zeckhauser. 1978. *A Primer for Policy Analysis.*
New York: Norton.

Stone, Deborah A. 1988. *Policy Paradox and Political Reason.* Glenville, IL:
Scott, Foresman/Little, Brown.

———. 1993. "Clinical Authority in the Construction of Citizenship." In
Public Policies for Democracy. Helen Ingram and Stephen Rathgeb
Smith (Eds.). 1993. Washington, DC: Brookings Institution.

Stone, John, and Stephen Mennell (eds). 1980. *Alexis De Tocqueville: on
Democracy, Revolution, and Society: Selected Writings.* Chicago: University of Chicago Press.

Torgerson, Douglas. 1986. "Between Knowledge and Politics: Three Faces of
Policy Analysis." *Policy Sciences.* Vol. 19, No. 1 (July). Pp. 33–60.

———. 1992. "Editorial: Priest and the Jester in the Policy Sciences: Developing the Focus of Inquiry." *Policy Sciences.* Vol. 25, No.3 (August).
Pp. 200–227.

———. 1993. "Power and Insight in Policy Discourse: Postpositivism and
Problem Definition." Paper presented to the Annual Meeting of the
American Political Science Association, New York. 1–4 September
1993.

Tribe, Laurence H. 1972. "Policy Analysis: Analysis or Ideology?" *Philosophy & Public Policy.* Vol. 2, No. 1 (Fall). Pp. 66–110.

Verba, Sidney. 1996. "The Citizen as Respondent: Sample Surveys and
American Democracy." *American Political Science Review.* Vol. 90,
No. 1 (March). Pp. 1–7.

———, Kay Lehman Schlozman, Henry Brady, and Norman H. Nie. 1993.
"Who Participates? What Do They Say?" *American Political Science
Review.* Vol. 87, No. 2 (June). Pp. 303–318.

———, Kay Lehman Schlozman, and Henry E. Brady. 1995. *Voice and
Equality: Civic Voluntarism in American Democracy.* Cambridge,
MA: Harvard University Press.

Warren, Mark. 1992. "Democratic Theory and Self Transformation." *American Political Science Review.* Vol. 86, No. 1 (March). Pp. 8–23.

———. 1996. "Deliberative Democracy and Authority." *American Political Science Review*. Vol. 90, No. 1 (March). Pp. 46–60.

Webber, Melvin M. 1978. "A Different Paradigm for Planning." In Robert W. Burchell and George Sternlieb (Eds.). 1978. *Planning Theory in the 1980's*. New Brunswick, NJ: Center for Urban Policy Research, Rutgers University.

Weber, Max. 1946. "Bureaucracy" In *From Max Weber: Essays in Sociology*. H. H. Gerth and C. Wright Mills (Eds. and Trans.). New York: Oxford University Press.

Weiss, Carol Hirschon. 1991. "Policy Research: Data, Ideas, or Arguments?" In Peter Wagner, Carol Hirschon Weiss, Björn Wittrock, and Hellmut Wollmann (Eds.). 1991. *Social Sciences and Modern States*. New York: Cambridge University Press.

White, Louise G. 1994. "Policy Analysis as Discourse." *Journal of Policy Analysis and Management*. Vol. 13, No. 3 (Summer). Pp. 506–525.

Whittington, Dale, and Duncan MacRae Jr. 1986. "The Issue of Standing in Cost-Benefit Analysis." *Journal of Policy Analysis and Management*. Vol. 5, No. 4 (Summer). Pp. 665–682.

Wiggershaus, Rolf. 1994. *The Frankfurt School: Its History, Theories, and Political Significance*. Michael Robertson (Trans.). Cambridge, MA: MIT Press.

Wildavsky, Aaron. 1979. *Speaking Truth to Power: The Art and Craft of Policy Analysis*. Boston: Little, Brown.

Woodward, Robert. 1994. *The Agenda*. New York: Simon & Schuster.

Yankelovich, Daniel. 1991. *Coming to Public Judgment: Making Democracy Work in a Complex World*. Syracuse, NY: Syracuse University Press.

———. 1994. "How Changes in the Economy Are Reshaping American Values." In Henry J. Aaron, Thomas E. Mann, and Timothy Taylor (Eds.). 1994. *Values and Public Policy*. Washington, DC: Brookings Institution.

Yanow, Dvora. 1995a. "Built Space as a Story: The Policy Stories that Buildings Tell." *Policy Studies Journal*. Vol. 23, No. 3 (Fall). Pp. 407–422.

———. 1995b. "Editorial: Practices of Policy Interpretation." *Policy Sciences*. Vol. 28, No. 2 (May). Pp. 111–126.

Zetterbaum, Marvin. 1967. *Tocqueville and the Problem of Democracy*. Stanford, CA: Stanford University Press.

INDEX

157